MARKETING MATTERS IN LIFE AND IN BUSINESS

7 proven steps to success

Eli Zheleva

Marketing Matters In Life And In Business Copyright © 2018 by Eli Zheleva. All Rights Reserved.

All rights reserved. No part of this book may be reproduced in any form or by any electronic or mechanical means including information storage and retrieval systems, without permission in writing from the author. The only exception is by a reviewer, who may quote short excerpts in a review.

Cover designed by Luke Keil

Disclaimer: the author is not a financial advisor and so the information in the book should not be used without consulting a professional.

How to get in touch with the author:
- website at www.EliZheleva.com
- Facebook: Eli Zheleva
- LinkedIn: Eli Zheleva
- Twitter: @elizheleva

First Printing: December 2018
Independently published

ISBN-13: 978-1-98079-137-9

CONTENTS

WHAT CAN YOU GET OUT OF THIS BOOK? 1
MARKETING MIX OF NEW AGE MARKETING 4
PURPOSE & OUTCOMES 9
Worksheet 16
    Notes 17
POSITIVE COMMUNICATION 19
Worksheet 30
    Notes 31
PLANNING 33
Worksheet 46
    Notes 49
PARTICIPATION 51
Worksheet 57
    Notes 58
WIN, WIN, WIN 60
PROGRESS 62
Worksheet 72
    Notes 73
PRODUCTIVITY 74
Worksheet 94
    Notes 96
PRESENTATION 97
Worksheet 106
    Notes 107

HOW I MADE IT WORK?..109
TOOLS..138
EPILOGUE...148

WHAT CAN YOU GET OUT OF THIS BOOK?

This book is not only for marketers. It is for those who need a step-by-step guide on how to get what you want from life. It is also for those who are already working on getting that and want to sanity check your doings.

This book showcases the marketing skillset in a different way. It teaches you how to make use of today's technology and automation tools and software to optimise your life. It will explain why marketing matters in business and in your personal life.

Every good marketer should already know and be applying the information in this book. My experience shows that this is not always the case. Many people get stuck in the technicalities and don't step back to look at the bigger picture. I've been a marketer for 10 years and have worked with hundreds of people.

WHAT CAN YOU GET OUT OF THIS BOOK?

It has always scared me when people who manage paid campaigns, can't manage their own finances. In marketing we talk about optimisation a lot. Optimising the user's journey on a site, the site speed, the campaign budget, the conversions. But we don't look at how those tactics can help us optimise our lives.

In this book, I've done this for you. I've reduced the jargon usage, the technical elements and have given examples you can relate to.

After reading this book, you will have a clearer understanding of what it is you want in life. You might even be surprised at the result. You will also learn how to think beyond what you have and manage projects bigger than your current limitations.

After reading the book you will have used strategies which you can apply in any area of your life. The knowledge will help you improve your personal and professional life.

After each chapter, you will find worksheets with guiding questions. They will help you follow the steps and get to the next level in your life. You can answer the questions in relation to any goal you may have, or anything you'd like to do in life – from setting up or expanding your business, planning a holiday, getting fitter, or even buying a property.

Once you've read the book and have answered the questions, you will know what to do next. This clarity will reduce your stress levels. You will create your own plans and strategies on how to have more control of your time. This will give you more time for the things that matter and to spend with people who matter.

See you in the next chapter!

MARKETING MIX OF NEW AGE MARKETING

Because the purpose of business is to create a customer, the business enterprise has two - and only two - basic functions: marketing and innovation. Marketing and innovation produce results; all the rest are costs. Marketing is the distinguishing, unique function of the business.

PETER DRUCKER

Every business needs marketing and innovation, and so does every person. If we didn't innovate in our lives we would be bored, or even worse - we won't live fulfilling lives.

The book is a case study of how re-defining the meaning of something (in this case marketing) can change the way you use it and the results you get out of it. That's why later in this book, I'll be referring to this new way of thinking as new age marketing.

In traditional marketing, there's a marketing mix. It is a set of the factors used to influence consumers to purchase a product or a service. Initially, it consisted of four Ps – price, product, place and promotion. In recent years, those have grown to seven Ps, now including processes, people and physical environment.

In this book, you won't read about those. I'm only mentioning them as a reference point to show you where I've got my inspiration from.

The mix of the new age marketing also has seven elements, but they are different.

1. Purpose and outcomes

To implement a successful marketing campaign for your business or for yourself, you need to know the purpose. You need to know not only what it is that needs to happen, but you need to know why. Why it is important to the client, or to you? What is the ultimate outcome?

Aligning the purpose with a passion makes the journey easier.

2. Positive communication

Communication has the power to make or break relationships. How you communicate with others will determine the end result. Whether you make business or friends, poor communication can get in the way. Knowing how to position your idea and viewpoint will change the outcome. It's the difference between presenting a problem or presenting an opportunity for improvement.

Whilst we find it easier to communicate with others, the way we treat ourselves in our minds is not always the best. If we talked to a friend or a business partner the way we talk to ourselves, it's possible that we would soon be alone.

3. Planning

For years now, marketers around the world have been using the PR Smith's SOSTAC® Plan. This is a planning framework that helps you to put structure around what it is you want to do and what's needed to achieve that. Not knowing what you want and having a positive mindset about it is not enough. Putting a plan in place will ensure you have a much higher chance of success.

4. Participation

Unless you take action, things won't happen. As Tony Robbins says "Knowledge is not power - it is potential power. Knowledge that you apply with heart, that's real power." Unless you take action, you won't make a change and you won't get the results that you want. Things will stay the same.

5. Progress

When you see the results of your effort, you are more motivated to keep going. But sometimes progress is not visible immediately. You need to learn how to identify the correct measures to track progress and how to record them.

Persistence simply means not giving up. Not giving up on what you want to do, not listening to others and not letting them impose their fears onto you. You need to learn how to interpret the feedback you'll get in a way that allows you to grow.

6. Productivity

Some people think that being productive means getting many things done. Productivity refers to getting the right things done. If what you do doesn't contribute to the end goal, do you need to do it? Improved productivity means getting closer to the goal with the least resources. You need to learn how to prioritise the tasks at hand, delegate work, and manage your energy.

7. Presentation

In both, personal and professional life, the way you present something will determine how well-received it is. And the way you present yourself at an interview, for example, could determine whether you'll get the job or not. The way you present your services to a potential client, will determine if they will become a client.

PURPOSE & OUTCOMES

People don't buy what you do; they buy why you do it. And what you do simply proves what you believe.

SIMON SINEK

Do you know what you want? Do you know why you want it? And is it possible that you have confused what you want with why you want it? If you say you want money so you can travel more, is it the money you want or is it the travel? Focusing on getting the money will require a certain set of actions, whilst focusing on getting the travel will require a different set. Answer the first question again and check that really you know what you want?

When it comes to goal setting, marketing provides a lot of structure and tools on how to ease the process. A management framework called OKR is a great example of this. OKR stands for Objectives and Key Results. In our case, we'll replace objectives with outcomes. Because as Tony Robbins says, you might not meet the objective, but you'll certainly get an outcome. Using this framework will help you be clearer on what the outcome is. The key results will help you define what that outcome means to you and how to get it. It's a framework that Google's team uses and if it's good for them, it's likely to be good for you.

Focusing on the outcome will give you more flexibility on how to get it. Often people focus on the means to the end, rather than the end itself. This means that they are ignoring the other ways in which they can achieve the same outcome. Also, if they haven't chosen a way of doing things with which they are comfortable, or confident in, they are likely to find excuses as to why the outcome they want is unachievable. The reality is that they limit themselves by focusing on the wrong thing.

When setting your goals in personal life and in business you need to make sure that you're not setting up yourself to fail. You know you've set yourself up to fail when reaching the goal doesn't give you the satisfaction you want. A good way to sanity check that is to know that you're focusing on the outcome, not on how you think you'll get it. Here's a real example for you to demonstrate how focusing on the task at hand won't always give you the outcome you desire. One day I came back from work I saw a little "sorry we missed you" card from Royal Mail. It said they wanted to drop off a parcel, but I wasn't there. This happened during the week I decided that I would go to the post office on a Saturday morning. I put it on my to-do list "go to the post office". On Saturday morning I was up at eight o'clock, the post office opened at 8:30 and I was on my way by 8:15. I was half way when I realised I didn't have my ID on me, and I knew they would need it. I went back home, got the ID, got the little "sorry we missed you" card and off I went again. Upon arriving at the post office there wasn't any space at the car park and I had to wait on five minutes for someone to leave. When I finally found a place to park, I joined the long queue. As the queue was progressing, I was catching up on emails on my phone. It was almost my turn and I put my phone away, which meant that I looked at the "sorry we missed you" card. Imagine my frustration and surprise when I saw that the box ticked was not "your parcel is at your local post office", but it's "your parcel is with your neighbour"! I went back home and picked up the parcel from my neighbour. That was an interesting reminder for me that I shouldn't have put "go to the post office" on my list. I should have put "pick up the parcel" instead. I wasted an hour of my day, but at least I didn't make a fool of myself in front of the Post Office staff.

One of the reasons people don't feel happy and fulfilled is because they don't reach their goals. They don't reach them because they have poor goal setting standards. The good news is that this can be changed, as with many things in life. The marketing skillset lends itself nicely again by giving us SMART goals. SMART only means Specific, Measurable, Achievable, Relevant and Timely.

Specific

Having specific goals will significantly improve the chance of you getting what you want. If you're not specific enough, how do you know that you don't already have it. That's why whilst "being happy" is a great outcome, it is vague as a goal. Being specific about your goals means that you can define what happiness means to you. Whilst you need to be specific about what you want, it can be beneficial to be specific about what you don't want. You may have heard the story of King Midas who wanted everything he touched to turn to gold. But if you remember, he ended up turning those he loves into gold, as well.

When it comes to clarifying the outcome you want, be specific about what you want to happen, and what are you committed to doing. Be specific about who you need to become to get that outcome. In business terms, if you want to have 200 more clients, think about what your business needs to do to attract those clients. Do you need to expand your product range? Do you need to invest more into your marketing? Do you need to create more events?

Everything you do needs to have a purpose. Don't be mistaken that the purpose should be linked to a monetary value. The purpose is that thing you ultimately want, and as such it can be ambiguous. That's the O in the OKR system. The goals are the specific things that need to happen so you know that you're getting closer to that purpose. For example, a purpose can be to relax. That can come in different forms, so you can have as a goal – have a massage once a week, or go to the beach every day, or sleep in every Sunday.

Measurable

As well as being specific, the goal needs to be measurable. The easiest way to ensure that a goal is measurable is to assign a numeric value to it. You might want to get 200 customers for your business, or to be able to run 5K, or even to own a 3-bedroom house. As soon as you put a number on it, it's easier to measure the progress and to know where you stand in achieving your goal.

Achievable

Whilst anything is achievable, when thinking of your goals consider where you are at right now compared to where you want to go. You need goals that stretch you, but don't stress you. If you have ambitious goals, be proud of yourself. Just be aware that setting the bar too high can take longer to achieve. This means that progress will be slower than you might liked thus you could give up prematurely, believing that what you want is never going to happen.

Relevant

The goals you set yourself must, when met, bring you closer to your ultimate outcome. It's important to stay focused, as there will be plenty of opportunities to do exciting things that are not aligned with your outcome. If you keep getting side-tracked, it will take you longer to get what you want. This, again, can lead to you adopting the false belief that what you want is not really possible. Make sure that at all times you do something that's aligned with your ultimate outcome.

Timely

Put an end date to all your goals. People are more efficient when they work to a deadline. Often, the closer the deadline gets, the more work people do. On the other hand, if you have goals that have no deadlines, there's no real incentive for you to get started with whatever you need to do. Ideally, the timeline for each goal should be three months. That's long enough to see some results, and short enough to keep your enthusiasm and focus on the task.

PURPOSE & OUTCOMES

WORKSHEET

What is the outcome you want?

....
....
....
....
....

What would it give you?

....
....
....
....
....

If you didn't have to work for money, what would you do?

....
....

....

....

....

If you couldn't fail, what would you do?

....

....

....

....

....

What are you passionate about?

....

....

....

....

....

NOTES

The purpose of the questions is to help you clarify if your goal is what you want or it is the means to an end. If it's the latter, think about other ways to get the same outcome. Don't limit yourself in what you can do. If you had all the money, connections and time in the world, how would you have made it happen?

POSITIVE COMMUNICATION

*The world we have created is a product of our thinking;
it cannot be changed without changing our thinking.*

ALBERT EINSTEIN

How you approach things in life and in business will have an impact on the outcome. If you see something as a problem, then you are likely to want to ignore it or run away from it. If you see it as an opportunity, you will run towards it. People look for new opportunities, and never for new problems. The meaning we've attached to both words over the years has made it so that one is positive and the other is not. We have associated the word problem with something negative that is given to us, something we don't want and are not ready for. The opportunity, however, we embrace.

These words are the two sides of the same coin. Every problem is an opportunity to grow and to learn and everyone refers to growing and learning as a positive thing. So, a problem is only a problem if you see it as one.

Words and the meanings we attach to them shape our mindset and viewpoints. They either broaden our horizons or get us into a tunnel vision. How and which words you use will determine the quality of your business and personal relationships.

Digital marketers have even coined the phrase "content is king". Search engines need to see certain words on a page to show your site for those words. For example, if you sell roses and within the whole site there's not a single mention of the word roses, Google, Bing and other search engines won't know that your business is associated with roses. It's similar in life – if you're looking for a friend who can help you with DIY, you are likely to turn to those who have previously expressed some interest in or have said that they can do it. If your best friend is the best DIY person around, and you've never had the conversation, you wouldn't know to ask them. Have you been in a situation where you've looked for someone to help you with a task, and you ended up calling a professional because you didn't know how to do it? Then you share that experience with a friend and they tell you "oh, you should have asked me, I'm good at that stuff"? This is a prime example of the above principle, if you don't know that someone can do something, you won't consider them for the job. The same goes in business, if you're looking for someone who can help you with an Excel document, you'll turn to those whom you know are good at it.

It sounds simple, but here's the challenge. People often don't use the right words to describe themselves and don't give themselves credit for that which they are good at. This means that even if they are good at something, they won't mention it as they don't believe in their ability. You might know people who are great at something and are too humble to say it themselves. Even if you give them a compliment, they will not accept it. The more they deny it, the more you will stop associating them with this skill. The less they practice that skill, the less that skill will develop. This means that over time, their initial statement of "I'm not really that good" will become true.

In today's world, many people think that giving yourself credit for your skills, talent and dedication is a sign of arrogance. It is perceived as showing off. But let me tell you something, there's nothing wrong with showing off. If you have really done something, be proud of it, share it with the world. For example, on LinkedIn and on your CV, you must list your skills/capabilities and what you want people to find you for. It's only if you are taking credit for someone else's work, showing off is not acceptable.

Not accepting a compliment can have a positive side, too. As mentioned, anything can be seen as positive or negative. If you don't accept a compliment, that can be a sign that you have high standards. You may know that you can do better and genuinely believe that what others consider as a job well done, is only average. If that's the case, make sure that you don't undermine what you're doing. It's easy to only focus on what you want to achieve, and thus what you haven't yet done. Instead of focusing on what you want to achieve and how far you've come.

The words you say to yourself and others can be uplifting or disempowering. If you know how to use content in the right way, you will yield great results. If you know how to speak to people within your team or to your friends and family, you could address a problem before it even occurs.

Changing the focus of the situation by changing the words that describe it will lead to different results.

Opportunity is, of course, a very positive word. Everyone likes to have an opportunity, everyone likes the idea of being given a chance to do something, to create it or to change it. That's why the word opportunity triggers emotions in people that will inspire a completely different reaction to what the word, problem would. If the action is different, then you get different results. By changing a simple word we can change how someone perceives what you're saying. For example, instead of saying to a client or a friend "there is a problem with XYZ", you could say "there's an opportunity to improve XYZ". If you read between the lines, you'll see that you're not lying and there is something that needs to be addressed.

The first step to improve your mindset, thereby ensuring it helps you and it doesn't hinder you is to monitor your thinking. Everything that we see was initially someone's thought. The idea was in someone's head as a thought. The person then considered it and voiced it. Words are stronger than thoughts, because they have a different dimension, i.e. sound. After saying it out loud, the person took action and with the action they got the result.

Often people stop at the thinking part. One of the main reasons for this is the noise surrounding that thought. As soon as an idea sneaks in, many people are quick to come up with reasons why it won't work.

Whilst we don't necessarily have control over the thoughts that get into our minds, we have the power to decide which ones we entertain. We can also choose which ones to voice. It's vital to make sure we don't put ourselves down. Mistakes happen, no one is perfect, so it's possible that you have done something you're not proud of. Blaming yourself for what's happening in your life is not productive. Taking ownership of it is. Look at where you are at, and objectively think of why that might be. See what setbacks you've had and focus on learning from them.

Learning how to change the meaning you attach to situations, and to value yourself will come across in all areas of life. Your business success is a reflection on your personal success. If you know your purpose and have the right mindset, you are more likely to succeed than someone who knows what they want and has a list of reasons as to why they won't get it.

Next time when you spill the milk, burn your shirt while ironing, or do something that prompts you to say to yourself "you're such an idiot", don't do it. Instead, change it to "I'll do better next time". As with the client example earlier, you're not ignoring the fact that something didn't go to plan. Instead, you look at what you can do better next time and focus on that. To start with, you might find that you don't believe what you're saying, but as with anything in life, if you continue doing it for long enough, it will become a habit. Having the habit of seeing the positive in every situation will serve you well your whole life. Next time you are harsh on yourself, think if that's something you would say to your best friend, or to a child. If the answer is "no", then you shouldn't say it to yourself either. We're our own worst critics and are quick to judge things we do wrong. Yet we are patient when it comes to others. Think about how many friends would stick around if you talked to them the way you talk to yourself. Most likely not many.

Marketers are right. Content is king. It can make or break anything – people, relationships, businesses, even the user journey on a website!

How you react to certain situations is often a learned behaviour. There is a trigger and then a reaction. The reaction is based on the meaning you've assigned to the trigger. If every time you spill some milk you tell yourself off, then you'll become even more agitated when that happens. However, you can re-train yourself to smile every time that happens and that way you won't let it affect your day. That's why it's important to know which words to use, when to use them and how to make the most of them.

In marketing we work with clients all the time. Some are more challenging than others. As expected, those who are challenging we naturally don't want to talk to. Where possible, we delay conversations, or send an email. When we finally initiate the conversation, we do it with resentment. Based on previous experience, where we have not had a positive outcome we are now conditioned to believe that it will be the same in the future. Have you been in a situation, where you have a relationship like this with a client? You're not making much progress in your work because they're not giving you a chance and they keep interfering? Then all of a sudden, someone you work with covers for you when you're out of the office and says the client is great and signed off the changes you wanted. How is that even possible? The answer is simple. Your colleague didn't have the backstory that you had. They haven't experienced your frustrations and so they approached the client the way you approach new clients – with eagerness and enthusiasm. When you've worked with a client for a while and you keep getting the same responses, don't get frustrated. Try a different approach. Use words to shift the focus on something else that will be more valuable to the client. Think of ways in which you can add value to their business, forget all the past frustrations and how you can improve the relationship. Again, don't see talking and working with the client as a burden, see it as an opportunity for you to turn things around. Calling the client when frustrated, even if you don't let that show, won't drive the relationship forward. It will not allow you to see their viewpoint and other ways to meet their goals. A useful reminder is when clients are being difficult. It suggests there's no trust in the relationship. This could be the case because they have had bad experiences in the past. That's not your fault and it's not an excuse for them to behave this way, however, it's a good perspective to have. Focusing on how to gain their trust will definitely improve the outcome. Your actions will be different to what they are when you feel as if you're firefighting all the time.

Visualisations whether intentional or not, are a powerful tool. It's clear in the previous example that when you start a conversation with hesitance, you're setting yourself for a negative outcome. You need to genuinely and actively think of ways you can build a rapport with your client. Before getting in touch with the client, take a minute or two to think through how you want the conversation to go, not how you think it will. Don't focus on the fact that they're not co-operative. You don't know what else is happening in their life. They might be going through a difficult time in their personal life. Again, that is not an excuse, but it can provide context.

The kids who need the most love will often ask for it in the most unloving ways.

Russell Barkley

A vital part of good communication is praise. Praise is not something we should expect others to give us. It's more important for us to give ourselves praise and to recognise the efforts that we put in and the results we're getting. After all, we're the only people who know how much we've done on a project. If we keep beating ourselves up, on a subconscious level our minds will start believing the things we tell ourselves.

Content is what convinces others to take or not to take an action. It's what makes people think about something and what evokes emotion. Many people think about content only as articles. Content is everything. This book is a piece of content, presentations are content, so are videos, images and every other type of communication verbal or non-verbal you can think of. Everything is content. Every thought is content. If you know how to deliver content, it will be your gracious King who is there to make things happen for you. If you don't know how to use content to your advantage, it will be the vicious King that deprives you of opportunities and slows your progress.

WORKSHEET

When was the last time you were upset/mad/sad?

....

....

....

....

....

What did you focus on? Did you beat yourself up for what happened, or did you think of what you could learn from the situations and get ideas on how to improve it?

....

....

....

....

If your child was in the same situation would what you have focused on be the same as above, or different?

....
....
....
....
....

Read the word below out loud and make a note of how you've read it.

opportunityisnowhere

....
....
....
....
....

NOTES

Are you someone who finds a solution to every problem, or finds a problem to every solution? Things happen, you have the power to decide how to interpret them.

When reading the word above, did you read it as "opportunity is now here" or "opportunity is nowhere"? Set yourself a calendar reminder in a week's time to read it again. Even if you've read it as "opportunity is nowhere", it will be harder to read it the same way again. This shows that once you see the opportunity, it's hard to unsee it.

Would you benefit from a change in perspective? If so, dedicate 10 minutes every day for priming. Priming is a routine Tony Robbins has created and has been doing for years. Priming yourself allows you to take control of what you focus on. What you focus on will then determine what you see. If you focus on the tough aspects of a challenge, you'll see it as a problem and won't proceed. If you focus on the good part, you'll see it as an opportunity and you'll embrace it and grow.

PLANNING

If you fail to plan, you are planning to fail.
BENJAMIN FRANKLIN

Planning is knowing what needs to be done, as well as when and by whom. Scheduling and accountability are key components of the successful planning system. Just putting things on paper with no deadlines and people responsible for implementing the actions, won't get you anywhere. When planning includes people's names against a set of actions, you need to make sure that the tasks and deadlines assigned stretch them, and not stress them. Having people working under a lot of stress is not productive. You want to make sure everyone feels like part of the team, and everyone understands the impact of their actions, and inactions to the bigger project. Show people that you value them and that their commitment is important to the organisation.

When planning and scheduling, think of the best sequence in which things must happen to make the biggest impact. Ideally, you need to write down different sequences on paper visualise the results. Do this with such detail and determination, as if each sequence is already the one you've all agreed upon. Ray Dalio shared in his book "Principles" that people often decide and then look at the data, instead of looking at the data and then deciding. When planning, be open-minded, and stress-test your ideas on paper, before starting with implementation. This will reduce the risk of doing something you haven't thought through.

Planning is something people underestimate. Too often planning seems like dead time. People don't take the time to plan, because they have things to do. In today's world we're used to being busy. Therefore, doing things on paper, which is often what planning is, is skipped. When you feel like you're becoming overwhelmed and pressure is getting to you, it is crucial to step back and plan. Otherwise, because you're so focused on the task at hand, you don't look at the bigger picture.

As mentioned in the previous chapters, if you focus on the task, and not the outcome, you might be missing out on an opportunity to get the same results faster.

There are two main things to consider when planning.

The first one is structure, which will help you stay on track. In your plan, you need to have guidelines, lists with goals, tasks and resources, as well as milestones to let you know you're on the right track. Planning is combining all the information you have on a project and putting a structure around it. If you don't have any guidelines and you don't know what milestones need to be reached, you're likely to end up doing ad-hoc tasks. They do happen, and sometimes you need to do them, but you need to be aware of how much time is spent on them vs how much time you spend on the things that really matter. You want to be doing things that, when you look back, have helped you make progress towards the big project instead of only doing sporadic tasks. Usually people who do more ad-hoc tasks and get side-tracked are those who don't have a written plan to follow.

The other key element of planning is pace. Often when you start a project you are excited about it, and you are all in. However, you start reaping the benefits of what you're doing and end up not having the time to carry on the initial plan. For example, if you want more sales for your business and you start attending events and do networking, soon you'll get more business. However, because now you need to look after the clients, you won't have the time to continue to build your pipeline. Think of how to scale the project before starting it.

A few years ago, Forbes shared the shocking statistics that 90% of start-ups fail. The four main reasons for that are: lack of focus, lack of clarity, lack of resources and lack of planning. Planning gives you the opportunity to put on paper what you anticipate would happen. It allows you to see through the development of the project or the company you work on. It helps you to forecast your involvement in the process and what else might be needed to make things happen. With a plan you can outline clearly what needs to happen and when. This then allows you to get the resources needed on time, even if you don't have them at the start of the project.

An important practical element of planning is writing down (on paper or in a digital format) what you want to achieve and what you will need to achieve it. Whilst you need to plan for multiple way to get to your goal, you also need to plan for unwanted situations. Planning means being prepared. Make sure you know what you'll do in case you run out of cash. What will that mean? Will that be the end of the business? Have you thought about how you could prevent that from happening? Be diligent, thorough and precise in your planning, thereby ensuring you get to execute the plan and the likelihood of things happening according to plan will be higher.

A good practice when planning is to overestimate how long things will take and how much they will cost. For example, if you know that realistically something will take one hour to complete, write down in the plan that it is going to take you two hours. If you think of something will cost you £100, put the cost as £150 in the plan. This will give you a buffer should you need it. Should anything unexpected show up, you will have the flexibility to better cater for it.

In recent years marketers have adopted a development framework called scrum. One of its fundamental principles is the idea of working in sprints (short time frame) to accomplish tasks. At the end of each sprint, you have a complete and usable part of the project. This helps embrace change which can happen along the way. Whist you may have the greatest and the most solid plan in the world, external changes can and do happen. Brexit happens. Trump happens. We live in a world of uncertainty, and funnily enough, the only constant thing is change. If your plan covers a timeline of a year or more, it's likely that half way through, some things might no longer be applicable. Technologies are developing at a rapid pace and that which is not available today to help accelerate your idea, could be available tomorrow. Using the scrum methodology will make your plan flexible and easier to adapt to changes. Sometimes those changes will work in your favour, and other times – they'll work against you. If you prepare how to react to change, regardless of its nature, that will put you ahead of the game. Often people don't prepare for change and panic when it happens, even though it might be beneficial to them. People can get stuck in their ways, because they are naturally scared of change.

When it comes to planning, don't only plan your actions, but plan your outlook as well. Plan what to focus on if things don't go the way you want. Plan what to focus on when things do go the way you want. Either way there's a risk of you losing yourself, either in your triumph or in your desperation. We've all heard of stories of lottery winners who end up broke a few years later. That happens because they are not mentally ready to have all that money. They never thought it would happen to them, although they kept playing the lottery. They didn't have a plan which they had carefully considered and written down. When we meet obstacles along the way, no one says we need to be joyous or excited about them. With proper planning though, we can choose to be reasonable and wise, which will be more productive in overcoming obstacles, than if we were chaotic and frustrated.

The antidote of stress is preparation. In marketing and in life it pays to be proactive, rather than reactive. If you're going on holiday and you don't plan what you need, you may find yourself searching for these things you need at the last moment, and thus forgetting something. Some people have gone to the airport and not had their passport on them, others – their sun lotions, and the biggest stress, of course, is for those who have forgotten their selfie stick!

The antidote of stress is planning.

Once you know what you want and why you want it, and you have the right mindset, you need to start planning.

If you don't design your own life plan, chances are you'll fall into someone else's plan. And guess what they have planned for you? Not much.

Jim Rohn

You need to put in the time and effort to be best placed to grab the opportunity that will arise in front of you or to deal with the challenge that might come your way. A crucial part of being prepared is being aware. Knowing where you are now, what resources you have and what you're lacking, will help you to identify what is needed and to obtain them for when you need them. In sports, athletes prepare all the time for a single race or a game, which is a reminder that unless we are constantly preparing, we won't be able to show our best when it matters.

For years now, marketers around the world have been using the PR Smith's SOSTAC® Plan. This is a planning framework that helps you to write an effective plan in a few minutes.

The acronym SOSTAC® stands for:

- **Situation analysis.** Find out where you are now. What resources you do and don't have. Which benchmarks you can use against which to measure progress?
- **Objectives.** Think about and answer the question, "what do you want to get". Think about your purpose and outcome, as well as how to make the objective a SMART one.

- **Strategy.** How will you attain the outcome you want? Don't limit yourself to thinking about what you can do to make it happen, but what can be done.
- **Tactics.** These are ways you will deliver on the strategy. Whilst the strategy is the broader idea of the route you'll take, the tactics are the specifics of how to do that.
- **Actions.** Specify what exactly needs to be done, as well as, by whom and when the deadline for it is. The key here is the accountability part.
- **Control.** Define how you'll track progress. If you've made your objective follow the SMART rule, it will have a number assigned to it. You can then compare how far you are from that number and if at the current rate you'll meet the objective within the timeframe you've set yourself.

To give you some context, here's an example of how this can work in business.

Situation analysis

You own (or are the marketing manager for) a leisure centre business that's been going for a few months and you want to increase number of people visiting. You have £5,000 budget and you need to know the most effective way to invest that money to get the highest return. There's no website for the business yet. Your ideal customers are aged between 18 and 30. You currently don't do any marketing activities and have £30,000 monthly revenue. The average spend per head currently is £10.

Objectives

Increase the monthly revenue figures by 10% in the next 90 days, i.e. get £3,000 more in that time.

Strategy

There are plenty of options on what the strategy can be. I've listed a few below for reference, and one will be chosen for the next steps. When choosing the strategy perform a SWOT analysis to identify the strengths, weaknesses, opportunities and threats for each of them.

- Targeting
- Objectives
- Positioning
- Partnerships
- Processes
- Sequence

- Integration
- Tactical tools
- Engagement

After doing the SWOT analysis, social media campaigns can yield the best return on investment. With them you can combine promotions and partnerships with other businesses, as well as paid advertising. Social media can be more powerful than local radio for the chosen demographics, and the loyalty scheme can be done online as well. Social media can also spread the budget (of £5,000) over the full timeline of the project. Other strategies are likely to use up the budget quicker thus not giving the campaign a chance to realise its potential.

Tactics

We've now decided that social media is what we'll focus on and the tactics will be:

- Run social media competitions
- Run social media loyalty schemes
- Run paid advertising
- Run content marketing campaigns on social media
- Use chatbots (the latest trend in social media marketing) to increase conversions.

Actions

Below is a list of that which specifically needs to be done, when and by whom.

- Chloe to create profiles on the main social media networks – Facebook, Instagram, Twitter in week 1.
- Coralie to boost posts on those platforms to reach the target audience - ongoing.
- Stacie to reach out to existing customers and ask them to engage with the company on social media in week 2.
- Stacie to reach out to potential business partners and identify opportunities for collaboration and cross-promotion on social media – ongoing.
- Tom to develop the way the loyalty programme will work, e.g. if people should tag themselves to get every 5th visit free, or will they get a free pint every time they tag themselves and a friend, etc. – week 2
- Liz to run a content marketing campaign for social media to use storytelling as an engaging sales tool -ongoing
- Chloe to run weekly competitions on social media
- Ben to create a chatbot to engage with people liking the page and share latest promotions – week 4 (once there's decent audience established)

Control

Check the revenue figures regularly to see if you're on track. You need £3,000 more revenue in the next 90 days. With the current average price per customer of £10, you need 34 more customers per day to hit the target.

WORKSHEET

Think about the outcome you wrote down in the first section and answer the following questions:

Where are you at in relation to that outcome?

....
....
....
....
....

What is the main objective?

....
....
....
....
....

Describe it in a SMART way. Look at the chapter Purpose and outcomes for reference.

....
....
....
....
....

How can you get it done? What's your strategy?

....
....
....
....
....

What are the tactics you will use to meet the objective? List what's needed to meet the objective. Don't' think about only what you can do, but what needs to be done.

....
....
....
....
....

Who is going to do what and when? What are the actions?

....

....

....

....

....

How will you know that you've met the objective, and if you're on track?

....

....

....

....

....

What can you do in 10 minutes each day that will contribute to the end goal?

....

....

....

....

....

What can you remove/reduce from your current daily activities to ensure you consistently have 10 minutes every day?

....

....

....

....

....

NOTES

In the situation analysis, be objective about where you are at. If needed, talk to others to sanity check that you are not just being optimistic. When setting up a goal, add numbers to make it measurable and specific. The deadline should be no longer than three months. If you set an overall goal for a longer period, you risk becoming sidetracked. It's OK to split the goal into different milestones to make it more measurable. For example, if your ideal goal is to be able to run a marathon, and you can only run 100 meters, it's likely that you will need more than six months training. However, when setting the goal, make sure that the increment from where you are now to where you want to be is relatively small and relates to a shorter period of time. You have a higher chance of succeeding if you have 12 goals for the year, than one big one. Having milestones that are just out of reach, but still visible will help pace you. Reaching the end goal won't seem like a scary thing, as you'll only focus on the smaller one at hand. The compound effect of reaching those goals, however, will result in reaching the bigger one without you necessarily realising how far you've gone.

PARTICIPATION

The way to get started is to quit talking and begin doing.
                                             WALT DISNEY

This is the shortest chapter, because by now you should have the knowledge of what to do and now it's a case of doing it. The key to doing that is to find the intrinsic motivation to act. If you've followed the exercises in the book, it should be easier to find it. By now, you should know your why, have a positive mindset and have put a plan together. If you don't have those things, it will be harder to get going, which will let procrastination sneak in. If you know your true purpose, procrastination should have no chance against you.

Procrastination is a form a fear. We find it in many areas of our lives and some people have become so good at it that they procrastinate on everything, to the point that people think they are lazy. The fact that you're procrastinating means that there's something you're unsure of, there's a fear of failure that's stopping you. How many times you were excited about a thing some would consider a bit reckless, or unsafe, but you still did it, because you had a passion for that?

For example, I have a fear of falling and avoid high and unstable places. For that reason, I have always been scared to do a sky dive. In my mind, there are only a few things that are worse than the free fall. For others, however, that's the best feeling one can experience – a feeling of freedom. For years I've wanted to do it but haven't had the guts. I was given an opportunity to do an indoor skydiving as a proof of concept for the real thing, but in the end I couldn't due to shoulder injuries. Phew! I now have a legitimate reason to justify to myself why I shouldn't do it. Having said that, I still play badminton, which is also not allowed because of those injuries. But why am I not procrastinating about getting back on the court? It's simply because I love the game. I have other injuries from badminton and I know there are risks in the game, but I still do it. Now that's a prime example of how our brains work – if we're afraid of something, we'll delay starting it and will come up with a million reasons why we shouldn't do it. As you saw, I even have a medical reason! That medical reason couldn't stop me doing the things I'm not afraid of though.

If you fear that you won't be able to do something, this is when you'll start procrastinating. Rarely do we hear about someone procrastinating going on holiday.

Procrastination can be redefined. We've now proven that it's linked to a fear and to perceived bad consequences. If that's the case, let change what we fear. Instead of fearing failure, invest that energy into the fear of missing out. Let's say you want to get fitter. You sign up for the gym and you go religiously the first month. Then you get off the rails. If you can't quit procrastinating, then procrastinate quitting. Fear that if you don't, you'll miss out on having more energy for the fun in life!

The more you delay something, the harder it will get to get going. Use Mel Robbins' 5-second rule and make things happen. Mel has explained it in and excellent way – watch her videos or buy her book on the topic. The simple idea, however, is this. The things you love doing, you'll have no problem taking part in. The things where you don't feel like you have all the resources for, are the things that you'll procrastinate on. From the moment you have an urge to do something, you have five seconds to take an action. The action shouldn't always be completing the task. Setting yourself a reminder, scheduling it or telling someone else you'll do it, is still a good start. When it comes to telling others, a good way to do something is by making a public commitment. The more people you tell that you're going to do something, the harder it is to get out of it. When I had the idea of writing this book, I started saying to everyone that I'll be writing a book. Then the next time I met those people they asked me how the book was going. This was a great incentive for me to get it done sooner rather than later.

People underestimate what 10 minutes could do for their lives. Warren Buffett, the greatest investor of all times, has said that the main contributing factor to his wealth is the compound interest. In life, the compound effect of consistently working on a goal even only 10 minutes a day will yield great results. And 10 minutes equate to just under 0.7% of your day. Now time is no longer an excuse. If you still struggle for time, read thoroughly the Productivity chapter, and you'll find how to take control of your time. If you say, and be honest with yourself at least, that you don't have 10 minutes every day, then your "why" is not big enough.

As 10 minutes is a short amount of time, you need to make sure that you dedicate them every day to your goal. Otherwise, you will miss out on the compound effect. If you train a muscle, it will grow stronger with consistent workouts. You will find that the results will be better if you train every day for a shorter period of time, than if you trained twice a month for excessive hours. Work in increments. The antidote to procrastination as Tony Robbins says is progress. You need to know that you're making progress to keep going. Otherwise, what's the point? The thing to remember is that sometimes progress is visible later, and you need to make sure you don't give up before you see it.

In life, there are two types of people – those who do well and those who dwell.

Eli Zheleva

In life, there are two types of people – those who do well, and those who dwell. You can't be both. People who don't take action on what they know, or what they want to find out, are unlikely to be fully satisfied with their lives. On the other hand, people who do well are those who have acted upon that knowledge. Regardless of how small or big the action is, they are moving and are building momentum.

Another reason people are not participating in their own success story is because they only look at the bigger picture. They see a big opportunity, or a big problem and are afraid of it. They automatically think that they won't be able to deal with it, because it's too big. You've probably heard that the easiest way to eat an elephant is one bite at a time. That's why consistently doing something for 10 minutes means that you will do small chunks of activities towards the main goal. And because they are small, you won't fear them, and you won't procrastinate on them. You will then incorporate the new habits into your routine. If something is a part of your routine, it's easier to keep it going. The compound effect of these small actions will have a life-changing effect.

WORKSHEET

What can you do today that will contribute to your big goal?

....
....
....
....
....

Give a few examples of things you have been procrastinating on.

....
....
....
....
....

What would be the consequence of you not doing those at all?

What do you fear? What's the worst that could happen if you did the thing you've been procrastinating on? How would you feel?

NOTES

When you don't feel like doing something, focus on the outcome. This is where you will find the motivation. That's why it's important to know why you're doing something. For example, there are not many people who enjoy working out because of the sweat and the physical fatigue. They overcome that initial thought and think of the long-term gains – fit body, full of energy and strength.

WIN, WIN, WIN

Congratulations to those of you who have gone this far in the book. I'd like to think that it's everyone who reads it, but statistics show that just under 50% of people read a full book, even if it's a best-seller.

My way to say thank you is to give you the opportunity to win a 7-week coaching programme with me. Every month, one lucky reader will be drawn at random and win the prize.

How to take part

Entering the draw is simple. All you need to do is to send an email to win@elizheleva.com with your feedback on the book – good or bad, short or long, I want to hear it all.

The prize

You will receive a 7-week coaching programme worth £1,999. I will work with you on a weekly basis to show you how to get to the next level. If your goal is a business one, I will teach you how to analyse the data and derive insights from it to make decisions that will improve your numbers. If you have a personal goal, I will work with you to help you become more confident, resourceful and more productive to reach the goal in the shortest possible time.

For those with attention to detail

The first one to report a typo or a grammar mistake in this book will get a 1h call with me. You decide on the topic of conversation. So think carefully where I would be able to add the most value to your life.

When you find the typo, send it to the email above. There will be page on www.elizheleva.com keeping a public record of what has been reported.

PROGRESS

If you're walking down the right path and you're willing to keep walking, eventually you'll make progress.

BARACK OBAMA

How do you know you're making progress? Are you sure that what you're doing is worth the effort? Either way, would you keep going?

Those are questions people ask themselves soon after they have started a new venture. Not surprisingly, often they have either not let enough time pass to see meaningful results, or they haven't defined how to measure those results. This leads to people prematurely giving up what they are doing and not reaping the benefits of their work.

Over the years I've worked on figuring out the answers myself and found that the key to all of them is awareness.

Awareness is seeing objectively what's happening and generally paying attention to your environment. Awareness is being a bit British and stating the obvious. A topic of the typical small talk conversation is the weather. The conversation goes like this:

Person A: Oh dear, it's raining again.

Person B: Oh yes, it is.

Conversation over. We should take a page from the Brits' book and apply it in our personal and business lives. Whilst stating the obvious can look pointless. It can be greatly beneficial. If you didn't know that it was raining, would you see the progress when the sun come out? You wouldn't have a comparison point.

If you don't know exactly where you are in life and in business, how do you know if you haven't got to where you want to be? If you don't know what's happening, how can you figure out what might be causing the ups and downs and thus what to avoid and what to get more of?

Benchmarking is a form of awareness. It is a value (not necessarily numerical) that we assign to something we're aware of. Below are a few examples:

- I can run 5K without getting tired
- I struggle to get out of bed
- My business is making me £100,000 a year
- My car's fuel consumption is 60 mpg

Knowing where you are now in relation to a specific goal will help you track your progress against it. If you didn't know how much money your business was making, you could set yourself a goal to get £80,000 per year. The example above shows that this will be an irrelevant goal, as we've already surpassed it. At the same time, if we wanted to get £300,000 per year, we would need to be aware of what is required to make that happen. We would then need to assess what resources we have available to dedicate to that goal, if any. Having too many unknowns can jeopardise the project's success. We can't be aware of everything at all times, but we can decide to start being aware of things regarding a project we're working on.

To run a successful project, you need to be aware. Find out and ideally, write down, what skills and resources you have to complete the project. Then, more importantly, write down what you are lacking. Once you've analysed what you're lacking, you can decide if you have the time and the drive to acquire the skill, or you can look for someone who already has it. When people have higher awareness on a subject, we say that they have a flair for it. And the dictionary's definition for flair is "a special or instinctive aptitude or ability for doing something well". If you are aware, you have a higher chance of doing something well than a person who doesn't have the information you do.

Being aware is a learned process. Just like a muscle, you need to train it every day. A good starting point for training your awareness is to be aware of your strengths and weaknesses. The important thing is to be objective about those. Write down a list of top 10 things that you consider yourself good at, and top 10 that you can improve on.

When analysing yourself, you need to be honest. This can be challenging, as a part of our brain does not always allow that to happen. It associates the honesty with pain. It's feels that by admitting that there are things you're not good at, it is admitting that you have failed, which is not the case. In fact, the people who have made the biggest progress in life are those who have recognised and constantly recognised their weaknesses and the areas they need to improve.

If you're not sure that your judgement is objective, ask a few people who know you well to list their perception of your strengths and weaknesses. Make sure those people will be honest with you, as well and won't just tell you things you want to hear. Then compare the lists and see if you've missed something. When only looking at 10 things, it's possible that you wouldn't have mentioned the 10 things that are on their lists. This is even more beneficial, because you end up with a more extensive list. When I've done this I found that many people in my business environment thought one of my strength was patience. They said that I was calm under pressure and had the patience to resolve the problem and to listen to all parties. Thinking about it, that was the case, however, I would have never considered myself a patient person. In personal life, up until a few years ago, I've been mostly hot-headed and that is how I would have described myself. Hearing that from others allowed me to revisit the behaviour in my personal life, only to find out that I have indeed calmed down and have more patience. By doing this exercise you can find out how you are perceived and you can compare it with the blueprint you hold of yourself. If you feel that you're confident, but people have said you should improve on that, you need to focus on how you project it. If you don't have the knowledge of what people think, you wouldn't know what to work on.

Reflection is a good way to practice awareness. Analysing a situation after it has happened, will allow you to see it from a different perspective. Things can look one way when we're in the middle of the situation, and a different way – once it's all over. Knowing what has caused an argument, will help you avoid it in the future.

When you are aware of where you've started and work on a task, even if it doesn't seem like it's giving you an immediate return on investment, think about the long-term gains. Know if what you're doing is a tactical or a strategic action. Tactical actions often relate to short-term actions that show results quicker. Strategic actions are those we take over time for a long-lasting benefit. Either way, it all starts with being aware.

Awareness in personal life

I started running in the mornings just after New Year. As we know, one of the reasons New Year's resolutions usually don't work is because life gets in the way. I didn't take up running as a New Year's resolution and was determined to prevent life from getting in the way. I decided to game the system of how my brain works. I was aware of what kind of excuses I would come up with and I destroyed them one at a time. The first excuse I knew I'd have was the cold weather. After all, early January is still winter and running along the seafront can be chilly. I bought myself gloves. I went for a run once and then realised that as the air was too cold, my throat started to hurt. Instead of giving up there and then, I bought myself a balaclava. The other excuse I had was that it was dark in the mornings – when I say mornings think 5:30am. I counteracted that with running on the main roads with street lamps. As I live in the UK, it was inevitable that one of the excuses that might pop up at some point is that it's raining. That I prevented by getting myself a waterproof jacket.

Do you see the pattern here? I know myself well and I am aware of what I might tell myself when it's time to go for that run. That's why I made sure that I couldn't make those excuses. When you don't have any excuses, then you must do whatever it is you need to do. That's why often people are quick to find reasons why they can't or won't do something even if they know it will be beneficial to them. Even if I wasn't aware of all the excuses to start with, I had to actively be aware of when they come up. I'd then acknowledge them and come up with a solution on winning against them.

Awareness in business

Are your marketing activities and your business making you money or losing you money? You need to know your numbers to know if you're making progress, or if you're moving backwards.

It's a crime that in today's digital world some business owners still don't know which parts of the business are the most profitable! I've talked to business owners in different countries and there are still people who run big organisations that don't know which product is bringing them the most money. Of course, they don't know which products lose them money, either. Some companies introduce new product ranges because they want to see an increase in revenue. However, they have failed to recognise the fact that the product that costs them the most to produce is losing them money. This means that to contribute to the bottom line, they can discontinue the non-profitable product and re-invest the money from it into those that work. They can then see an increase in revenue without having to expand the current product range. You need to focus on tackling the problem at its core, rather than thinking of a way to mask it.

If you can see the progress, it's easier to keep going with a task. Seeing that you're moving in the right direction is motivation in itself. You rarely see people who want to do something, they know it's good for them, when they see it working, and give up. The rare cases when that happens is when the progress is not quick enough. However, with a change in focus and vocabulary you can still present that progress rate in a better light. For example, when tracking the progress, make sure that you look at the by-product of what you're doing and how far you've progressed. If your goal is to be able to run 5K, as you're building up to it, recognise the fact that you have more energy because of the physical exercise, you focus more easily and you are calmer. This means that even if it takes you months to build up to run that distance, along the way, what you're doing is still moving you forward in other areas.

Data analysis

Modern marketing is all about data. Data-driven business insights and strategies are something you should expect from a reputable marketing company / professional. Data analysis can eliminate the guesswork and will get you better results. When tracking the performance of any activities against a specific objective, make sure to use the correct metrics. For example, if you want to make your business more profitable, looking at the money coming into your account alone won't be indicative of whether you're getting closer to your goal or not. If your costs have increased, and the net profit is lower, it's a false economy. Never look at data in isolation. Analyse each relevant metric in relation to the other relevant metrics.

WORKSHEET

How do you know if you're on track?

....
....
....
....
....

What metrics are you using to track the progress?

....
....
....
....
....

Is it possible that even when the metric you're tracking reaches its target, you are still not happy?

....

....

....

....

....

NOTES

When tracking progress, it's key to make sure you're using the right metrics. Answering the third question often helps clarifying the purpose. For example, let's say a marketing client says that they want 500 visitors to their site, but once the goal is reached the client can still be unhappy. Why? Because none of those visitors became a lead. This suggests that the main outcome is to have more leads rather than traffic. You know you're tracking the progress towards a correct goal when meeting that goal will make you happy.

PRODUCTIVITY

The key is not to prioritize what's on your schedule, but to schedule your priorities.

STEPHEN COVEY

Productivity is making the biggest progress within the shortest timeframe. Being productive means getting the right things done. It's not to be busy being busy. Doing many things, if not on track, won't make you more productive. It also won't help reduce stress and won't get you closer to reaching your goals. Organising your day and knowing what needs to be done, and by whom are some of the keys elements. There are five main areas of productivity that are directly within your control.

Lists management

Lists tend to have a bad reputation. This is mainly because of people's ability to manage lists, what goes in them and the way they're referred to. Often people think of lists as "to do" lists. They are associated with chores or things someone has told us to do. There's no surprise that no one will be excited to get a list of such things. If there's no excitement you'll resent looking at the list, let alone working on the tasks. When a task on the list is not completed, things can easily go out of control. Many tasks get piled on top of each other, and there's no excitement there either.

The first step to improve your list management is to change how you refer to the lists. Lists should be seen as assistants, because that's fundamentally what they are. Lists are the assistants that will help you get from point A to point B. They are what will keep you focused, on track and sane.

It's interesting that we tend to overestimate what we can remember. Instead of writing down whatever comes to our minds, we think we'll remember it. What we're failing to remember though is that there are only so many pieces of information our brains can store. Studies show that every day 60,000-90,000 thoughts cross our minds. Most days we have the same 15,000 thoughts. It's optimistic to think we can retain even 1% of that information. The chances can be significantly increased if we write things down as and when they arise. There's no point in adding information to your brain that's not relevant to the task at hand. Even if you don't think actively about something, unless it's written down, this thing is still taking up space in your brain's RAM.

For example, nowadays we can rarely remember off the top of our heads the numbers of three people in our phone contact list. But surely, we have more than three people we regularly call. At the same time, we try to remember shopping lists, things that happen at work, things that we need to do on our personal projects. The easiest solution to make sure we don't feel overwhelmed but on top of things is to write everything down. We should capture every thought we have on paper or even better, in an app. The challenge with writing things down on paper is that there's no reminder option. Also, based on my personal experience, paper can easily be misplaced or thrown away by mistake. It's unlikely you'll do that to your phone or laptop. Well, I'd like to think it's unlikely for that to happen.

In my marketing career, I've worked with many businesses, most of which use different apps for the same thing. That's how

I've got to test many free and paid apps for time and project management. The one I've found mostly useful is Toodledo. Toodledo is easy to use, has a browser-based version and a mobile app. You can attach files, have subtasks, and collaborate with people. The thing I like the most about Toodledo, which other apps are missing, is the ability to allocate time for each task. Once you've planned your week, allocating the anticipated time a task will take is a must. This is an easy way to make sure you're not allocating too many things for the same day. It's easy to think that a task will take us only 10 minutes and so we'll add it to the list. But then a similar task comes up and we add it to the list. We keep adding small, or sometimes bigger tasks, and we end up adding tasks that physically will take more time than the day has. As we're used to thinking that being productive is ticking many boxes off, we can't bear the thought of having only a few things on our list. However, it's better to have a few things and to do them than to have many small ones, which keep getting missed.

I have lists for many things, not to say for everything. Sometimes I think I go overboard with those lists, but after all I'd rather know I have things written down and can refer to them when I'm ready. This saves me having to keep everything in my mind. For example, I have a list of books and articles that I'd like to read, a list of tasks that need to be done for different projects, a list with places I'd like to visit and so on.

Remember people and experiences everything else write down.

Eli Zheleva

Many people think that when they add something to the list, they need to do it as soon as possible. This is not the case at all. One of the reasons to add things to a list is to be able to prioritise them. You need to recognise that you can't effectively prioritise the tasks required to complete a project, if you haven't listed all the tasks that need to be done in the first place. Listing everything will give you a clearer understanding of the different things that would take your time and attention. Things could often look scarier, bigger and more complex than they are if you only keep them in your minds. If you break them down to their integral parts, things suddenly become a lot easier to comprehend and thus a lot easier to action. Therefore, physically listing everything and anything needed for a project boosts productivity. By actioning the individual tasks, the percentage of project completion increases and it's easier to track the progress you make. Seeing progress is one of the keys to success. If you don't see the progress you're making or do things that don't get you closer to the ultimate goal, or God forbid you don't have an ultimate goal, then it doesn't matter how many tasks you tick off.

A paradox of today's society is that people want to be seen as being busy because this gives them a sense of significance. If someone is seen to be busy, they are perceived to be important. But that's a trap you don't want to fall into. You'll be better off having a few tasks on your immediate "to do" list. Better still, those "to do" items should be outcomes, rather than tasks. For example, instead of having "go to the gym", put "increase energy levels" or "get fitter". Focusing on the outcomes allows you to be more flexible with the tasks that you will use to reach the outcome. If you want to get fitter, there are many ways to do that – so if you don't have enough time to go to the gym, you can do a shorter workout at home and have the same results.

When adding things to your lists, it helps to use exciting and empowering words. Using positive language will entice you to do the task and will make you look forward to doing it. Using such words might sound unnatural and silly to start with and that's OK. It is proven that if you set yourself a higher target and you don't fully reach it, you are likely to have gone further if you had set a lower one. Therefore, if you just put "go to the gym" on your list, you're likely to do just that. If you, however, put "increase energy levels", going to the gym can still be something you do. The emotion attached to the task is likely to inspire you to do more than that, you can consciously drink more water that day, or have a healthier meal. The ripple effect of outcome-based approach will give you greater results.

It's similar in marketing, if you put "get the client a mention on a national newspaper", you'll work on doing that. If you had "make the client a though leader within their industry", you get many more options on how to do that. When you have a choice of options, you are likely to be more inclined to work on getting that outcome.

Going back to Toodledo's functions, I'd strongly recommend you use the time allocation column. We often underestimate how long things would take or we overestimate how much we will be able to achieve in a day. Ultimately this leads to frustration and reduces our productivity. Get into the habit of giving yourself a buffer when allocating the time tasks will take. If you know for a fact that something will take you two hours to complete, allocate two and a half hours instead. That way you account for any interruptions that might occur. Of course, at the end of the day, if you find yourself having some spare time, take a task from tomorrow's list, or a backlog you have and work on that.

Equally, if you have not managed to complete all tasks for the day, make sure to reschedule them accordingly. Don't leave them as overdue, as the thought of this adds stress even it's on a subconscious level.

Prioritisation

Once you have a complete list of what needs to be done on a project, you need to start prioritising. You are not productive if you're doing things for the sake of doing them.

You don't want to start with the thing that would take you the least amount of time and will have the least impact. Equally, you don't want to start with the biggest task, drain yourself and lose the willingness to continue with the project. Mind you, if you have a task so time-consuming that it puts you off then you have done something wrong. You should never have such tasks.

Each task should be broken down into smaller chunks that are easy to digest and easy to work with. Here's how to sanity check if your lists have a hidden mammoth task. Once you've allocated the time you think each task would take, check if there are any that will take your more than two hours. If so, look for ways to break it down into smaller parts.

When assessing tasks, you need to look for those that are relevant and important because some of them might be important but not relevant to the task at hand. Sometimes you're better off doing something that is less important, and it's more relevant.

Having lists and prioritising them is important at the start of any personal project or business venture. Many people I've spoken to are afraid to start their own business because they don't know if they could manage. They don't have timelines to work with and no clear prioritisation of tasks that need to be completed. Before starting to invest money, invest time into research and planning. Don't limit yourself to what you can currently do. All you need to start with is a list of the ingredients that will help you make it happen. If you don't know what those are, start googling or ask people who already have similar businesses. People fear the unknown and rightly so. Proper planning can mitigate the risk involved in realising a business idea.

I'd like to think that you've come up with an idea no one else has had, however, it's possible that others have already done something similar. Initial recommended Google search will be "how to start a business" or "how to start a XYZ business". Have a look at the first 10 articles, combine the recommendations and list them. Now you have a good starting point. Some of the actions involved might be – register the business name, get business cards, find an office, go to networking events, etc.

When you have the list, start prioritising. Here are a couple of key questions to get you started:

- Do I need an accountant at the start of the business or would I need them in a year's time when I need to do my taxes?
- Do I need an office, or could I operate remotely or in the client's office?
- Do I need a website first or to go to networking events?

The answers to those questions will vary depending on the industry you operate in, the business model and perhaps even the country in which you live.

If you're not sure, by looking at the list, what the most important tasks are use the comparison method. For example, let's say you have tasks A, B and C on your list. Compare A to B and if A is more important, compare A to C. If A is more important again, then A is the one that needs to happen first. Continue by comparing each task to the others in the list until you have a weighing system that shows you which task "won" the most comparisons.

Delegation

The next key to productivity is delegation. Many people think that as soon as they add something to a list, that's something for them to do, but that's not true. You can have a list of things for someone else to do. The task for you may be to check the quality of the work delivered, whilst not doing the work itself.

Delegating work shouldn't be a way to avoid responsibility or to pile stuff onto someone else. It's effectively managing your time. Admittedly, there will be things that you wouldn't be the best person for anyway. The fact that you know you need to do them, doesn't make you qualified to do them. Always be on the lookout for time swap opportunities. For example, with marketing I prefer technical tasks to outreach. I can do outreach and have done it, but it will take me longer than some of the outreach specialists I've worked with. This means that if I need to do outreach and the outreach specialist needs some technical tasks done, it makes sense to swap the tasks. Instead of me spending 2h on outreach and my colleague spending 2h on the technical tasks, we can spend 1h on the thing we're good at. This way, I will get to do a task I enjoy and I know for a fact I'm better at, whilst regaining an hour my day. The same will go for my colleague. One can argue that I won't get any better at outreach if I keep swapping it. That is true, however, it's important to realise that we don't have to be good at everything. Find the things you do well and excel at them.

Acknowledge your strengths and weaknesses and see what you're good at. Talk to your friends, family, and colleagues about what they're good at. Then look for ways to exchange time that will be beneficial for all parties. Where possible, don't do tasks that someone else can do better and more quickly.

The more you climb the ladder of personal and professional success, the more you have to protect your time. Therefore, you need to be able to "clone" yourself and to trust that when you request something it will be done to your standards. How well a task is done depends on the person doing the task as well as how good your brief is. As a marketer I often had to do briefs for the journalist to write content for our clients' websites. Looking back, the times when I got what I wanted was when I was specific in my request. I asked them to use certain resources or focus on topic, etc. I learned that the more specific I was, the better results I got. It's the same in life. People don't have clear vision and goals on what they want to achieve and where they want to go. They then stress about the fact that they don't know what to do and are not making progress.

Don't judge people's performance based on your poor briefing skills. If you want to improve the quality of work someone delivers for you, first look at what you can improve. Is your briefing system up to scratch? Are the processes you use and the way you communicate with people working effectively? Are you asking for and getting feedback? When giving people feedback, it's not a case of telling them off. To start with, you need to make sure you understand why they have done the job in that way instead of what you anticipated. Maybe you didn't say that you expected the delivery within a set deadline, or in a set format. It's always a good idea to create a process whereby after you write a brief, the person doing the work explains to you what they plan to do. That way if you feel that there is something regarding the change, before the actual work commences, this can be agreed upon. Doing this will save you hassle later on and no time will be wasted in delivering something you wouldn't be happy with. The sooner you get into the habit of giving tasks away, the quicker you will make progress in your projects. Delegation is a muscle that needs to be trained. If you don't do it with small tasks, you won't do it with bigger ones either. This means that your stress levels are likely to increase over time and you will burn out.

If we can pay for something and have our time back to work on more important tasks, we'll progress in our projects faster than someone who keeps all tasks to themselves. Time is something that we can't get back. We can find a fiver on the street, but we can't find five minutes on the street, you can only lose them there.

Focus

One of the other ways to increase productivity is to stay focused. As expected, that's easier said than done. Being focused depends on many factors. One of them is your energy levels. If you haven't managed to sleep well or are poorly, it's harder to keep focused regardless of your good intentions. Looking after your physiology will increase the chances of being productive.

Another thing that can affect your productivity is how you deal with distractions. Nowadays everything demands our attention - social media, websites, ads, people, etc. This makes staying focused harder. Therefore, you need to make a conscious effort to learn how to stay focused. To start with, note how long you can work on a task before looking at your phone, or emails, or talk to someone. If the answer is 10 minutes, set yourself a timer for 15 minutes and ignore everything and everyone for that time. You might find it useful to have headphones to block any noise out. The more you allocate those 15-minute focus slots, the more your brain will get used to focusing. Then you can increase the time to longer periods. Like every beginning, it might be hard to resist the temptation to look at your phone, so if needed put it aside or on silent mode. Silent mode means just that. Having your phone on vibration won't do the job, as your attention can still drift away if you feel it buzzing. When a phone buzzes it suggests someone has expressed an interest in us. They have messaged us, they have liked something we'd posted, they have retweeted something we'd shared, and they have engaged with us in some way. Whilst this is great you need to remember is that this notification will be there 15 minutes later. It will be there at the end of the day as well. And if something is urgent people would have called you. When you are working on reducing distractions, have a policy with yourself and share it with others. If there's something urgent they should call you. But other than that, you could take a little longer to get back to their messages, and they shouldn't be offended because teaching yourself how to focus is an investment in yourself. We can't control the thoughts that get into our minds, however we can control which ones we will pay attention to and entertain.

Focusing in an office environment is even more challenging because even if no one is talking to you, people talking amongst themselves can be a distraction. Having headphones could be considered as anti-social behaviour, but if you explain the reasoning behind it, your team will understand this. Again, if something is urgent then your colleagues should come and talk to you. You'll find that often if you ask people to contact you only if something is urgent, suddenly the distractions from others reduce. This makes you start questioning why people distract you in the first place.

I'm not talking about social interactions. Part of going to work is to connect with people. At the same time, if you keep staying late because you can't focus and can't complete your tasks that needs to be addressed.

The reason I recommend implementing the learnings from this book in the order they are shown is because each section complements the previous one. By now you should have clarified for yourself what you really want and have a detailed plan on how to get it. Knowing what benefits getting that outcome will get you, and better still – knowing what you'll miss out on if you don't get that outcome, can help you stay on track.

Focusing on one thing, however, shouldn't mean excluding other things completely. Instead, it's about balance. You can use the Pareto (80/20) principle. 80% of your focus should be on top 20% percent of activities. Adhering to this principle is especially important when it comes to marketing. In our industry, it's easy to get sidetracked as new technologies and tactics appear all the time. You need to be aware of those and maybe test them, but you shouldn't keep changing what you do just because there's new hype.

If you spend 80% of the time on things that you know have worked, and 20% on innovation, you're covering all bases.

Time management

When it comes to time management, first you need to know where your time goes. For example, think of the types of tasks that take up most of your time. Is that work, family commitments, sports, social media/TV, studying, etc.? Think about the percentage split between those. When you know that, you can look into each category and see if there's a way to optimise your time within them. You might even find that there's a category that's not serving you and you can replace it with another one that does.

A few years ago, I was feeling constantly overwhelemed as I never had enough time in the day to do the things I wanted to do. I thought I knew what was taking up my time, but it turned out I didn't. It wasn't until one day I downloaded an app called TimeTune and realised what was happening. The app allows you to track and optimise your time. When I got it, I put down everytihng I do on a usual week and allocated that time in a few categories. For two weeks afterwards, I started tracking my weeks in real-time. When I analysed the data, I was shocked to find that I was spending 22 hours every week in commuting! In my mock-up week, I have only allocated 10 hours. It's not a rocket science to figure out that there were 12 hours in my week

I thought I had, and didn't. Straight away I realised why the week was never enough for what I wanted to do. I then re-adjusted my days to fit the actual available time I had in a week. It worked wonders. My stress levels dramatically reduced and my self-appreciation increased. At that time, I was feeling down, as I was thinking that I couldn't get things done as quickly as I used to. Being aware of what had happened helped me regain my confidence that and realise I was in fact still doing more than the average person. I had just miscalculated the amount of time I had to play with.

When I focused on optimising my time, I looked for ways to combine tasks and to get some more time back. That was the time when I started listening to audiobooks. Amazon's Audible has revolutionised my life! I love books, but because of my busy schedule for the five years beforehand, I had only read university textbooks related to my studies, and there is more to life than computing and IT. In the last year alone, I've listened to more than 50 books. I can listen to books whilst commuting, cooking, cleaning and so on. I no longer have to tell myself that I don't read because I don't have the time. Business books, like this one, are a source of systemised information that helps you to get a distilled version of the knowledge someone has acquired over decades. Many people prefer printed books. Whilst the experience of falling asleep with a book on your chest is great, I found that I can listen to books faster than I can read. This means that if it takes me 10h to read a book, I could listen to it for 6h instead. Also, as mentioned, I can listen to it whilst doing something else as well. This means that I don't have to find 10 extra hours to read the book. Instead, I merge it into activities that I'm doing anyway. The other benefit I found with audiobooks is that they allow my eyes to rest. I stare at my laptop or phone screen for a big part of the day, every day, so being able to enjoy a good book without putting extra strain on my eyes is welcome.

WORKSHEET

Create a list of everything and anything you need to do this week.

....

....

....

....

....

Look at the tasks and turn them into outcomes. Choose those outcomes that you can use different tactics for and get the same results.

....

....

....

....

....

Prioritise the list of outcomes by comparing each to the other one using the technique outlined in this chapter.

....
....
....
....
....

Who can you contact if you don't have all the skills needed to complete the tasks on your list?

....
....
....
....
....

List which skills can you trade with someone if you can't pay them for their time, so they can still help you with their project.

....
....
....
....
....

NOTES

Find out what your biggest challenges are when it comes to productivity. Use the comparison method and identify which one you need to focus on first. Also, don't forget that you need to know what has to happen, but shouldn't always be the person to make it happen. Even if you don't have the authority or resources to delegate tasks, think creatively and come up with ways to trade your time for someone else's.

PRESENTATION

There are many ways to be wealthy. Don't limit yourself to money. Have more love, gratitude, knowledge...

ELI ZHELEVA

Marketing matters. It is something every business and every person needs. The marketing skillset is so comprehensive and universal that once you learn it, you can apply it in every industry, every country and every language.

If you want to make it in life (whatever that might mean for you), if you want to succeed and if you want to be satisfied with who you are, following the steps in this book will help you achieve that.

In every step of your life, you need to know how to market yourself, and your business, and here's how to do it.

You need to know how to present yourself. When you go to an interview, you need to show someone within a short period of time that you could bring value to the organisation. When you meet a new person and again you need to show they can bring value in their life. When thinking of value, don't only think of the monetary side of things. The value could be emotional, spiritual or just being present for someone.

Be authentic

Be true to yourself. Be who you are all of the time. Don't change who you are because you think that someone might not like you. If they don't, then they are not worth your time. It's better and more productive to be yourself all the time in front of a few people, than being what many expect from you and trying to constantly keep up the roles and masks. Whenever you are about to do something when you're amongst others, ask yourself if you would do it the same way when you're on your own. In many situations, people criticise others for something that they themselves do when they are on their own. Ask yourself, who you are when no one is watching? If you dance in the rain when you're on your own, why would you not do that when others are around?

Focus on adding value

Adding value, to me, means to make something better, to improve it. There are endless ways to improve the same thing or situation. Even if you can't change the whole entity, think of ways to improve its components. In marketing, and in life, things always evolve. As soon as you publish v1 of a website, or yourself, you need to think of ways to improve that, often based on the changes in environment and feedback from others.

Select who you spend time with

You need to be associated with the right people - authorities, influences, professionals and industry bodies within your area. Choose your circle wisely as the perception people have for you can be down to who you work with and learn from. Being recognised by people who are already established leaders give you credibility. Those people will be able to confirm that your skills to the desired standards. I often hear people asking how to get into the circles of the authorities and how to convince them that they are the right person. If you've just started to market yourself, not many people will know about you. It's a catch 22 situation – you need to be associated with reputable people to establish yourself, and those people as already established want to associate themselves with other reputable people. Being in this situation is a great reminder of the importance of the previous two points. Be true to yourself and your mission. Be authentic. Be committed. Then think about the value you can bring to those people. If you doubt that you can bring any value to their lives, that doubt will come across in your communication and the outcome is likely not to be what you want. However, if you believe that you can help those people in some way, the introductory conversations will be far easier.

Learn how to communicate well

Communicating well includes knowing what to say and when to say it; it's just as important to know when not to say anything. Listening to others is something we're losing the ability to do and it's causing us our business and personal relationships. We're often too quick to come to conclusions before hearing the other side. In his book "How to Win Friends and Influence People", Dale Carnegie has a lot of practical tips on how to do that. Listening is a key one, along with becoming genuinely interested in others. Talking about their interests instead of yours, and making the other party feel important. Acknowledging someone's viewpoint, validating what they already know and giving them a sense of significance goes a long way.

In addition to the verbal communication, think of the non-verbal, as well. Think about what your body language says. Smile at others, look them in the eyes, open up and see how much more receptive they will be of your ideas.

Be honest

We've all said a lie or two in our lives, and perhaps we've all been caught lying once or twice. Let's face it, lying is not worth the hassle. Again, sometimes we're changing our story, because our egos don't want to admit we've messed up. Owning up to what we've done is an honourable thing.

I'll hold my hand up to say that in the past I've received emails from clients asking for a report I've not had the time to send yet. To avoid admitting that, as I thought the client would be upset, I'd say we'd had troubles with the emails and maybe my email has got lost. There were times when emails were indeed playing up, but sometimes I was creating a story to avoid confrontation. It's not something I'm proud of doing, but I'm proud of learning from it. I realised that sometimes clients were just asking for an update, but because I knew I hadn't delivered, I thought I would be in trouble.

Identify your strengths

There are debates, on A) if you need to identify your weaknesses and work on fixing them, or B) to see what you're good at and excel at it. My recommendation is to do the latter. Focusing on improving what you are already good at will get you greater results. I've always told people that the things I'm not good at are the things I don't want to be good at, and I believe every word of it. If I'm not good at something that means that I don't have the desire and a big enough reason to want to improve. This means that I won't put in the necessary time and effort to make progress in that area, let alone going the extra mile. When something interests me and I have a reason to want to do it, I immerse myself in it and as expected, get good at it.

Knowing what you're good at and excelling at it, therefore, is easier. The fact that you've become good at it suggests that you enjoy it and/or you find it easy. If you decide to focus on improving your weaknesses, you are likely to find yourself reluctant to start the improvement process. This means that your focus and commitment levels will drop. In summary, if you spend 10 hours on improving what you're already good at and 10 hours on working on your weaknesses, the improvement rates will be better in the former scenario.

Be consistent

You have probably heard the saying "How you do anything is how you do everything". People's perception of how you do things might be based on a single interaction they have had with you. If you overlook the details and the small tasks, you might not be trusted with a bigger project. It's important to deal with all projects, no matter how small or big, with the same attention, dedication and passion. Effort counts more than the outcome. The outcome can be influenced by external factors and you don't always have full control over it. You have full control over yourself though and can decide how much effort to put into what you do. Answer the question "Who are you when no one is looking?". Do you take shortcuts because there's no boss around, does your motivation reduce if the project at hand is not big or exciting? My dad asked me once why I was indicating when driving in the early hours and no one was around. I told him that I'm not doing it for others, as much as I'm doing it out of habit and because that's the right thing to do. The more you do something, the more it becomes a part of who you are. If you keep taking shortcuts when you're not supervised, you can sabotage your future success. If you decide to have your own business one day, this habit will show up and it will be a costly lesson. That's why I urge you to consistently do your best in any and every area of your life, as that's how you'll build good habits which will help you in the long run.

Speak up

Being a good listener doesn't mean we should not speak up for what you believe in and let others lead the way. Speaking up can be daunting, but we need to remember that it is so because of our egos. Our egos fear rejection, failure and confrontation, which is why it will help you come up with stories as to what would happen if you spoke up. Speaking up doesn't mean being rude or disrespectful to others. As long as you adhere to that idea, there's nothing bad that would happen. If anything, people get a lot of brownie points if they can stand up for themselves. This is a highly valued quality in business and the sooner you start showing it, the sooner you'll become more respected in the eyes of others.

PRESENTATION

WORKSHEET

List three things you can do that will add value to the people around you?

....

....

....

....

....

List three things you can do that will add value to your business or the company you work for.

....

....

....

....

....

What would stop you doing those things (both personal and professional)?

....
....
....
....
....

What can you do to pre-empt whatever might arise, to ensure you will do those things?

....
....
....
....
....

NOTES

When you stop focusing on your ego, i.e. on how you think you look, how you think people will perceive what you say, etc. and focus on adding value, your life will change. Do things with a genuine interest and aim to help others and enrich them. How people will react to what you do, or what they will think is a reflection on their world, and not a reflection on you. You may say something that one will find tremendous value in, yet someone else will curse you for it.

HOW I MADE IT WORK?

After reading this book, there will be three types of people. The first type are people who have already come up with a few excuses and reasons as to why the information is not applicable to them. The second type are the people who want to try and are not quite sure how it will apply to their lives. And the third type, are the people who have already taken something on board and have a plan on how to implement it.

It's the first and second types of people that I want to dedicate this part of the book to. I will give you a couple of examples of how I've used those steps and have transformed various areas of my life. Hopefully after you see a real-life example, it will become clearer why applying these steps, in this order will help you reach your life goals.

Buying a property with no money

Almost 10 years ago, I read the first personal development book – "The 4-hour work week" by Tim Ferriss. Since then I've read "Rich dad, poor dad" by Robert Kiyosaki, "Think and grow rich" by Napoleon Hill, and "The monk who sold his Ferrari" by Robin Sharma. I had the pleasure to meet Robin in 2017 at a seminar in London. At that point I already knew how simple things could be. And simple doesn't always mean easy. I don't live in a delirious world with no reality check, and not all things are easy for me.

Reading the above books and then some over the years has widened my horizon and has made me realise that things are possible regardless of the resources you have. The knowledge I acquired from those books has shortened the distance between my situation at the time and reaching my goals. The main reason for writing this book is to help you do the same.

Initially, I didn't apply everything from each book. In fact, I still haven't applied all the knowledge, but I constantly add to my skill set and improve what I do and how I do it, and I encourage you to do the same. Unless you try it, you will not know if your current way of doing things is the most effective and efficient to achieve the outcomes you want.

Here's how Robert Kiyosaki's book got me onto the property ladder. In his book "Rich dad, poor dad", Robert is talking about financial principles that are not taught at school and are not part of the regular curriculum. Therefore, they often remain misunderstood, unexplored and unused. One of those principles is how to make money with no money. Sounds great, doesn't it?

I moved to the UK in 2010 and since then I wanted to buy a property. Like many, however, I didn't have money for the deposit. I could afford the monthly payments, but I didn't have the upfront lump sum to put upfront. That's a situation in which many people currently are. Further in this chapter I explain how I made it work. Please note, that I'm not a financial advisor and what has worked for me might not be the right approach for you. I'm just sharing my journey to give you an idea of how to look beyond your limitations, financial or other.

It's not the lack of resources that gets you down but it's the

lack of resourcefulness.

Tony Robbins

When I decided I wanted a property, I didn't mind whether it was a house or a flat, although I would have preferred it to be a house. To start with, I just wanted to get onto the property ladder and that was going to be a good first step for me. With all my good intentions, I only had £2,000 in my account and thought that getting a property might be a challenge. Unlike many people that didn't make me give up on the idea. Instead, I started to research the options and I decided that do a sanity check on paper. I got a piece of paper where I physically wrote down the numbers required for the purchase. In the digital era we live in, we really have no excuse not to get better at the things we want to get better at. There's plethora of information available and 80% of it is available for free, at our fingertips. It's just a case of going to Google and searching for what we need.

Before starting the search, I defined what property I was going for. This was crucial, as that was going to determine the resources needed to make the transaction. Then I had to find out the costs. Of course, I needed to pay for the property itself, so I had to figure out what other costs were involved. I needed to know how much I would be able to fund, and who to ask for the money. Getting a mortgage was an obvious thing, but with so many options, I had to see which product would work best for me. I had to review the difference in the interest rates. There were other things to consider and very quickly, I made a list of those. As soon as I made the list of things the next steps became clearer. The list was as follows:

- Find a 2-bedroom property within my current area up to £100,000
- Find out how much money the bank will give me for the mortgage based on my financial situation at the time
- Find out what the repayments would be on the mortgage
- Find out cost for utility bills
- Get a quote for solicitor's fees
- Get a quote for mortgage advisor's fees
- Find out if I'll be able to get a £10,000 personal loan and what the repayments would be
- Find out how much the estate agents' fees would be
- Find out what the stamp duty would be on a property with that price

After creating the list, I went to Google and I searched for mortgage calculators. A few minutes later, I had an estimate of how much money the bank would lend me. I knew those figures were subject to change and credit checks, but I needed a rough idea on whether it's worth me proceeding with the transaction.

At the time, my rent was £500 per month for a 1-bedroom flat and I figured that if I could have a lower mortgage, I could make it work.

After a bit of online research, I found that the mortgage interest rate depends mainly on the deposit and the credit score of the applicant. At the time, I didn't know what my credit score was, and I signed up for Experian. I used their paid service for a few months to gain a better understanding of how realistic my goal was. It turned out that I had a good credit score, so it was more a case of having a decent size deposit. I found that whilst 5% deposit is the minimum required, it bumps up the mortgage interest rate significantly higher. Putting 10% down gives a much better interest rate. If the deposit is increased to 15%, the interest rate is even better. Funnily enough, after my second property purchase, I found that putting more than 15% deposit doesn't really have a bearing on the interest rate. This means that even if you have the money to put down, it might be better to stick to 15%. I hope you don't mind me reminding you again that I'm not a financial professional, so don't take my word as gospel, but be mindful of my findings and check how they relate to your situation.

As mentioned earlier, I only had £2,000 in the bank, so I needed to fund the deposit somehow. To make it a bit easier, I decided to go with 10%, as opposed to the optimum 15%. If I were to get a property worth £100,000, I needed to find £10,000. Using the paid version of Experian allowed me to find out how my credit score fluctuated during the years and I found some patterns in those movements. I found that once a credit application is made, the credit score goes down a few points. It then recovers after a few months, and after six months, that credit application is no longer impacting the score. The partial credit score recovery happens after three months. What you need to be aware of, if you aren't already, is that the credit applications impact your score.

The credit score system is black and white. It doesn't care about how much you requested to borrow, it doesn't care about whether you took the loan or not, it only cares about the fact that you have requested to see if you could afford the loan. If you have asked several companies for a mortgage quote and all of them do a credit check, you're likely to see a big drop in your score. After the first request, your credit rating would have dropped, then after the second, it would have dropped even further and then after the third one, it would have plummeted.

Experian's system is just that, a system. If the system records that you have applied for a £10,000 loan with three different lenders, it "thinks" that you need £30,000, rather than just £10,000. I learned this this the hard way - my credit score was ruined by a car dealership when I wanted to get finance for a new car. What I didn't realise at the time was that the sales person had requested five quotes in two days and thus my credit went from "very good" to "poor". I only made the connection when I wanted to get a new phone contract a few months later for £20 per month and was denied due to poor credit score. You can imagine my shock when I knew I hadn't got any products on a lease that would have done that. I then found out that whether I accept the quote or not, doesn't matter, what affects the credit score are the number of applications. I hope you learn from my mistakes.

I checked using an online calculator that the repayment on a £10,000 loan would be £130 per month. The mortgage calculator showed me that if I was to get a mortgage for £90,000, the repayment would be £430. This meant that the sum of repaying both would be £60 more than what I was paying at the time. I could comfortably afford the extra payment and so, I decided to start the process.

The first step was to get the loan for the deposit. I got that in August 2014 and decided to wait for at least three months before I apply for the mortgage. I had decided that I would pay the loan off for a couple of months, and when I got the mortgage offer, I would see if I was to proceed. What you need to remember is that you need to minimise the risk you take. At that point, I had the loan and was repaying it for a few months, which was something I could afford. Then in October, I found a property I was happy with – a 2-bedroom maisonette for £91,000. This meant that I needed a mortgage for £81,000. I applied for it and as mentioned earlier, I could afford the monthly repayment. I had decided that if the number was out of my reach, I would return the loan (I made sure there were no early repayment charges) and I would have only lost £50 or so in interest for the few months I had the loan. I would have then waited for another three or six months for my credit score to recover and would have applied for the loan again, and a few months later – I would have done the mortgage application. And I would have repeated this process until the conditions were in my favour.

If you decide to try this, you need to be aware that not all banks accept borrowed deposits. Make sure you consult with your mortgage advisor what options you would have if you did that. Bear in mind that my mortgage was a single application, so if two people apply for the mortgage, in principle, it should be easier to get it. Banks see more security when more than one person is responsible for the mortgage repayment. Because if one of them can no longer afford the repayments, there's a back-up plan.

As you can see, it makes sense to check the numbers on paper before you proceed with any applications. The key is to know what you can afford and to stick to that. You want to stretch yourself, not stress yourself. If you're being realistic with the calculations, you can sanity check the numbers with someone else.

Once I got the numbers for the mortgage and the loan, I checked the utility bills, the solicitor and mortgage advisor fees, the council tax and stamp duty. I made sure that I could afford all of those and wouldn't end up paying a lot more per month than I was paying at the time.

As soon as I moved in I started thinking about how to sell it and make money. That was in December 2014. In the summer of 2016 a friend of mine was getting married in Spain and I went there for the wedding. I booked my stay in Malaga for seven days, even though the wedding and the BBQ the night before would have taken only two days.

Although I knew a few of the wedding guests I decided to book a room on my own. I wanted to have some *me* time to do some reflection and to set my own goals for the next two to five years. This was one of the most profound times in my life. I became increasingly aware of what I was doing, what I could improve and where I'd like to see myself going forward.

During that reflection time, I applied my marketing, project management and planning skills to plan my life. I remembered again why marketing matters. I looked at my personal goals and approached them with the same enthusiasm, creativity and commitment I would apply to a client's project.

During that trip I set four goals in different aspects of my life. For each one of them I answered four questions:

- **What do I want?** This was the top-level outcome I wanted to get.
- **What does that mean?** I put specifics of what it is I wanted, so I could recognise it once I achieved it. When it comes to goals, every marketer knows that goals should be SMART. And if you've read the book carefully enough, you'd also know what that means.

- **What do I need to do to make it happen?** I listed everything I thought at the time was needed to help me reach that goal.
- **How much time per week do I need to allocate to know I'm on track?** I wanted to know what time commitment I will need, so I could plan my time accordingly to allow for working on each goal.

One of the goals on that list was to buy a house. I've always lived in a flat and always wanted to have a house with a garden. I would have gladly bought a house with the first purchase, I just couldn't afford it at the time. That's why I decided this time to make it happen. Do you remember how I used a piece of paper the first time to plan things? Well guess what I used this time? You're right – another piece of paper. Here's how I answered the questions on the piece of paper:

- **What do I want?** A house with a garden.
- **What does it mean?** I wanted a house with two bedrooms and two receptions or three bedrooms and one reception. Basically, I wanted another room because before getting onto the property ladder I was renting place with my sister. We were living in two rooms – a living room and a bedroom. Then when we moved to the maisonette we had

two bedrooms and a living room – that's three rooms. Again, I thought that if we were moving to a new house, it might as well be a little bit bigger.

- **What do I need to do to make it happen?** As usual, I listed all the things that had to be considered. The key was to work out the numbers. If with the first purchase, I only had two thousand pounds in the bank, this time I only had five hundred pounds! I needed to find out the following:
    o how much money I still owed on the mortgage for the apartment;
    o how much money the mortgage lender will give me for a new mortgage;
    o how much money I need for a deposit;
    o how much money I need to pay solicitors' fees;
    o how much money I need to put for the stamp duty and all other legal things, etc.

Finding the answers to the above gave me a clear idea whether I would be able to pursue this or needed to hold fire. Initially, I wanted to remortgage the maisonette and with the money I could get out of the deal to put a deposit on the house and then to rent out the maisonette. I'm ambitious, aren't I! Because of changes in the stamp duty a few years ago, I would have ended up paying a lot more in legal fees. It would have been a stretch and if something went wrong, I would have found myself with two properties on which I wouldn't be able to keep up the payments. Therefore, to be more realistic and more comfortable with the deal, I decided to sell the maisonette and just get the house. During the process of selling the maisonette, it turned out that it had quite a few issues, so having to sell it was a blessing in disguise. I was privileged to have excellent solicitors who handled all the stress on my behalf!

- **How much time per week do I need to allocate to know I'm on track?** I needed to know the total time it would take me to tick all the boxes and to have all the answers before I could start the process. Although purchasing a property is a big deal, you need to realise that most of the work is done by your team. The solicitors, mortgage advisors and other professionals working with you. This means that the time it will take you to do the things on the list will be a lot less than you think. You need to authorise your team to do their respective jobs. The most time-consuming thing for you will be to arrange viewings and choose a place where you want to live. As with both my purchases I was specific about what I wanted, it took only a couple of viewings before I found the property I wanted. I'm a satisficer. I knew what I wanted, I found it, I got it. End of story.

In his book "The paradox of choice", Barry Schwartz splits people into two main types – satisficers and maximisers. Satisficers are those who make a decision once their criteria are met. That doesn't mean that they will settle for less than what they deserve, in fact often the criteria are high. However, as soon as the criteria are met, they'll take action. This is what happened with me – I knew the specifics of what I wanted and the house that ticked all the boxes (which happened to be the third one I viewed) is the one where I live now. Because of my quick decision making and delegating most of the work, it took me four hours buy a house and to sell the maisonette.

This was a good realisation for me, as it put things into perspective. We often look at a big project, get excited about the opportunities and then get scared. Because it's too big, our brains get overwhelmed and we start thinking we can't deal with it. The solution is simple – write things down.

When you do that, you allow yourself to fully comprehend the complexity and the simplicity of the project. This works with opportunities and problems. Sometimes we think that a problem is bigger than it is because we haven't taken the time to dissect it and see what small steps we can take to overcome it.

When we write things down we can get the scope of the project. We can see what will take the most time to complete, what tools and resources are required, etc. At that point, we'll be able to assess whether we have those resources and if not - whether we know someone who has them. It's vital to remember that you don't have to do it all. It's a case of you knowing everything that needs to be done and finding the right people to do it. I can hear straight away the more skeptical of you saying that you can't afford to pay someone to do the work for you. Here's an idea for you – don't limit yourself to a monetary exchange only. Think about what you can give to that person or what you could give to someone else who could then give back to this person. Bartering is still a part of today's world, so use it to your advantage.

Here's what I did earlier this year. When I moved into the house, I needed a gas cooker. The guy who came to install it and I got talking and he mentioned to me that he wanted to update his website. A few months later, when I needed a boiler service, I thought I'd get in touch with him. I offered to update his website in exchange to him doing the boiler service. It took him an hour to do the service and it took me as long to create him a basic WordPress site. And so, I didn't pay anything for the service and he didn't pay anything for the website. I have a serviced boiler and he has now more enquiries.

Think of what you can do for others and don't put yourself down. Don't think that because that thing is not your career, you can't help someone with it. If you have passion for something and you have done it for more than 100 hours it's likely that your level of understanding can be greater than someone else's. There are many ways in which you could trade your time; and sometimes your part of the arrangement might be just introducing the person who will be helping you to someone who could help them. Don't limit yourself to the material things you have. The purpose of this book is to remind you that knowing what you want and having the right mindset and strategy will help you make things happen. You'll be pleasantly surprised to find out that things can be a lot easier than you think.

Becoming an international speaker

September 2013 was the first time I attended the biggest digital search conference in the UK, BrightonSEO. Before going to the conference, I decided to write an article about "How to be a great conference speaker". I reached out to a few of the speakers at the conference and asked each of them the same questions. Not all of them replied, but those who did, shared some excellent advice. On the day of the conference I made sure I introduced myself. The two friendliest speakers I met were Lukasz Zelezny and Dawn Anderson. Both are amazing speakers and it was great to be able to associate myself with them. We then connected on social media and I started following their journey. A few weeks after the conference, Lukasz posted a photo from another conference, in Milan. Then from another one – in the US, and he never stopped travelling. That's when I had a breakthrough. I realised that I'd love to do what he's doing. He was travelling the world, talking about things he loves and believes in, and he gets paid for it!

I decided that if someone whose native language is not English can ace English-speaking conferences, so can I. And this is where it all began, so thank you, Lukasz!

HOW I MADE IT WORK?

I decided that I'd like to do a TED talk one day, and I started to work backwards on figuring out what I need do to make that happen. Not everyone gets invited to do a TED talk. Those who do are people who have contributed to society in some way and are known for doing so. I've always been a people's person and always have contributed on a local scale, but I wasn't known on a global level. Of course, to do a TED talk I had to be a great speaker as well, and that could only happen through training and practice. But who would let me speak if I don't know how to speak? I then found out about Toastmasters International. This is a platform that helps you build your public speaking skills.

Over the years, I improved my speaking and presentation skills, I met hundreds of people at conferences, exchanged ideas, and continued with my mission.

I've also signed up to be a translator for TED talks. I decided that I can contribute, before I am given an opportunity to shine. I've translated a few talks from English to Bulgarian.

Note that when I first had the idea of becoming a TED speaker, I didn't focus on the fact that I didn't have the relevant skills and experience. Instead, I focused on reverse-engineering the process and figured out what I could do to get a step closer to the goal. Rome wasn't built in a day. Don't be scared by your big goals, be excited about what your life is going to be once you reach them. Also, acknowledge how you'll grow as a person in the process.

To become a great speaker, I needed to have a great message to deliver. I've spent almost half of my life in marketing and I saw that as an excellent starting point. In the last few years I've been working with a life coach and I have become aware of how the marketing principles overlap with life. I found that marketing matters to everyone who wants to move forward in life and in business.

For a few years I had the idea of becoming a speaker in the back of my mind. I knew that to get people to listen to me, I needed to work on my personal brand first. During that trip to Spain for my friend's wedding, I put this as one of the goals. On the piece of paper, I answered the questions as follows:

- **What do I want?** I wanted to build my personal brand. I put this as a goal for the following two years.
- **What does it mean?** I wanted people to know my name and what I stand for. I wanted them to learn about the positive difference I want to make in the world and join me in that quest. To make the goal more specific, I decided that the first milestone will be to get 100 people

on average to search for my name every month. With the help of some marketing tools I could monitor the numbers and see if I'm on the right track. I also wanted people to see me as a trustworthy person and authority in the industry and to let me help them become their better selves.

- **What do I need to do to make it happen?** This was the question that took longer to answer. It was easier with the property, as there aren't many ways to check the stamp duty and to pay it. When it comes to marketing there are tens, if not even hundreds of ways to build a brand. Here are a few of the things that crossed my mind:
    - Create a social media campaign and use paid ads to promote myself
    - Create a website and write blogs and then get traffic via them
    - Collaborate with existing businesses
    - Do free trials of the services I offer
    - Go to networking events
    - Do something PR work, e.g. get involved with a charitable activity, etc.

I decided to go with a combination of a few of the above.

- **How much time per week do I need to allocate to know I'm on track?** I knew I needed at least four hours a week to write a blog, schedule promotion and do outreach.

Here are the details of how I made it work. I realised that if I appeared on reputable business websites or in the media, I would be perceived as an authoritative person. To do that though, those publications would need to see other articles I've written or that I've been featured elsewhere. I therefore focused on getting featured in smaller publications. Those smaller websites and blogs, however, don't want to feature any random person as they have a reputation to protect. Again, I needed to be able to show that I am trustworthy, and I know what I am doing. To do that I needed to do some outreach and to see who would be willing to write about me. I was sure I could add value to their readership, I just had to think of a way to prove that to someone who hadn't heard of me. In the end, I decided to speculate to accumulate.

As a marketer I have used many promotion tools over the years. I figured that if I wrote an article on a subject I'm passionate about and people shared it and I could use those stats in my outreach emails. That way, when I contact those publications, I could demonstrate that my articles get shares.

Then I could quite comfortably rather than making things up, say that my articles have been shared hundreds of times. I was open about using promotion tools and when doing the outreach, I mentioned that once the article on their site is published, I will allocate some resources to promote it. This would give exposure to the blogger and would add to my credibility. I knew I needed my own website as a platform to share my thoughts, realisations and learnings. I published a few articles on my own website, each of which got over 500 shares on Facebook and Twitter. I used Quuu Promote to get the social traction. This meant that if someone wanted to verify the numbers, they could. The shares are from real accounts, many of them even verified, showing that real people have read my article and have decided to spread the love. Then out of the blue I was invited to write for a new marketing/business website. The first article I wrote for them was about fear and was titled "Let's talk about the F-word". The article discussed how fear stops us from excelling in business and personal life. Using some clickbait in the title helped get that article hundreds of shares, as well. The website editor was happy with the engagement the article received and invited me to become a regular contributor to the site. That was the first milestone.

Once I had the numbers backing me up, I started to approach different publications saying: "I see that your blog is about marketing/business/life coaching/confidence, etc." and I believe that I could add value to your readers. Would you be willing to host an article that I've written?" In that initial email, I gave a list of articles I've written, plus the number of times each has been shared. They could then see that I am passionate about what I do, and the articles get exposure. That was free publicity for them. There is something interesting about ego. Whenever someone gets featured on a site, their ego prompts them to shout about that. Shouting about my articles on other websites was a part of my marketing plan anyway and I gladly went above and beyond to do that. The articles I wrote were educational and inspirational. I didn't use them as a platform to sell my services. I wanted people to read my articles and get value from them.

After a month or so of doing the above, I felt ready to up my game and get in touch with even more established websites, bloggers and even a radio show! All of those, I arranged via Twitter. Everyone has heard about Twitter, but not everyone knows about #journoreqest. The hashtag is often used by journalists, writers, event organisers who are looking for input from people that meet certain criteria. They might look for people with certain skills, or life experiences, or an opinion on a subject. These are mostly unpaid opportunities, sometimes the journalists will even offer you payment for your time. That's not at all why you should monitor #journorequest though. You need to follow the hashtag to see if someone is looking for you. It's easier to meet existing demand, than to generate it. This means that you are more likely to get your name in a bigger publication as a contributor to an article, than to have your own article there. I've had great success with #journorequest. I contributed to an article on Huffington Post. It was an article about why women should take up sports. I used to play badminton and that got me a mention and a photo! Now I can legitimately say that I've been on Huffington Post. Whilst it's not for sharing my business knowledge, it still sounds impressive. By using the #journorequest hashtag, I did an interview for Lady Like You and Kate On Thin Ice. Those sites featured me in my role as an entrepreneur. I had the opportunity to share my experience and journey to inspire other women to start their own business. The articles had positive feedback from the readers and that was a reassurance for me that I'm doing the right thing.

With #journorequest I got in touch with Women in Business radio show and was invited to be a guest in their studio. That was the first time I was on the radio in the UK and was a thrilling experience. The hosts made sure I was comfortable being on air. We had lots of fun during the interview discussing how to be more productive. We focused on how lists can help get our thoughts organised and how to be on top of our lists rather than under them.

I gained a lot of momentum with those collaborations and was then featured in Empowered Magazine. Thanks to that article, I was approached by a radio host in Texas. I was asked to do a radio interview for Global Voice Radio in March, as a part of a campaign for "Voices of Women". I again shared my story, my mission and some tips on how to get through challenging times.

It was again via Twitter that I also got an opportunity to present at two high profile women empowerment conferences. The organisers were looking for women who wanted to make a difference in the world and I got in touch straight away. I had a call with the main organiser and explained my business idea to her and how I've decided to combine marketing and life coaching. I talked about why marketing matters on a personal and professional level, even if people do not want to do marketing as such. When I was pitching myself to the organisers, I already had some online presence. By that time, I'd already increased the awareness for my brand. When looking at the stats, on average 20 people per month were looking for my name. I knew that I was getting closer to the first milestone!

As you can see, I started with nothing and quickly built up my local presence. I did it with no money, just with creativity and some marketing knowledge. There are many ways to get started. Unfortunately, there are twice as many excuses you can come up with that will prevent you from starting.

The only thing that will cost you a fortune are your excuses.

Everything else you can get for free.

Eli Zheleva

One of the reasons to share the details of how I started to build my brand is to show you that if you focus on it, you can do it. It doesn't matter what resources you have or you're lacking, your determination and passion are all that matter. The other reason to mention the publications and organisations that have helped me along the way is to thank them for believing in me.

The magazines and the radio shows were platforms to share my experience and expertise. Reaching their audiences has boosted my credibility and even self-confidence.

Now I'm able to raise the bar higher. My next step will be to pitch to the Entrepreneur, Forbes and Inc.com. Getting an article published on those sites will significantly increase my exposure due to their big readership. I know that before submitting an article idea to those publications, authors need to have on online portfolio. As explained above, I already have that and am well placed to be considered as a contributor.

TOOLS

In marketing, we use a plethora of tools. Many of them provide the same or similar information just with a different interface. Many of them have different ways of collecting data. Choosing the best ones for you will depend on the insights you will need to derive from the data and the format/layout in which you want the data to be presented to you.

I've listed below tools that have helped me my personal and professional life:

Google Sheets

Google Sheets is an online spreadsheet tool. You can use it the same way you use other spreadsheet tools. It helps you to do simple and complex calculations and visualise data. The good news is that it's free unlike Microsoft's products. There are plenty of fancy things you can do, e.g. translation, checking for valid addresses and sending emails with comments. Go to Loves Data's blog (https://www.lovesdata.com/blog/google-sheets-tips) to find more applications. I tend to use Google Sheets for my monthly financial planning. I know how much money will come in and how much will go out. Using Google Sheets helps manage better my money. It makes it simple to forecast how much money I will have in a few months, which allows me to know if I can afford something or not. And if not, what arrangements I can make to accommodate the anticipated extra outgoings.

Head to sheets.google.com to try Google Sheets.

Toodledo

This tool has revolutionised the way I structure my days. It helps me plan and reduces the stress in my life. I have now mastered how to use it, and made it work for me. Toodledo is a very simple tool, and through its simplicity, it has tremendous power. Go to www.toodledo.com, create a free account and start organising your day. As I have mentioned before, I have a lot of lists and Toodledo is where I store them. I like Toodledo because it has an app and a web interface. This means that as soon as I think of something, I can write it down straight away, as I always have my phone with me. Nowadays, I rarely use paper notes as that way I don't have to remember to look at the piece of paper and digitise it later. And if I don't add the tasks from the paper notes to the main list, they are likely to be overlooked. Having an app on my phone that syncs with the web interface make it easier for me. If I'm working or at home, I'm often in front of the laptop, and there I use the web interface. At all other times, even if I'm abroad, I use the app to keep on top of what needs to be done and who needs to do it. I add various ideas that may cross my mind. As mentioned before, I use lists not only for things that I need to do, but things that I want to follow-up on in the future. Adding them to the app, I know where to look for them when the time comes. As part of my productivity quest, I make sure to update Toodledo every day with the tasks for the day, plus how long I think each would take me.

F.lux

Ever notice how people texting at night have that eerie blue glow? Or wake up ready to write down the next great idea, and get blinded by your computer screen? During the day, computer screens look good—they're designed to look like the sun. But, at 9PM, 10PM, or 3AM, you probably shouldn't be looking at the sun. f.lux fixes this: it makes the colour of your computer's display adapt to the time of day, warm at night and like sunlight during the day. It's even possible that you're staying up too late because of your computer. You could use f.lux because it makes you sleep better, or you could just use it just because it makes your computer look better.

Go to www.justgetflux.com to download the app. It's free for personal use. Isn't that great?

Audible

Another piece of software that I use is Audible. Audible is an excellent tool allowing you to keep enriching yourself even if you are busy. Audible provides audio books are podcasts. Nowadays wherever we go, we have our phones with us. This means that we could listen to audiobooks everywhere. It is one of my favourite apps because before I discovered it I hadn't read a proper book for five years. All the books that I have read in that time were university textbooks. With Audible I now listen to books when I'm cooking, walking, commuting waiting for a friend, etc. I no longer need to pack a book for my travels and can combine the book with something else. Listening to books is better for my eyes as well. Being a marketer means that I spent a considerable amount of time staring at a screen.

Nowadays many people say they don't have time to read and I was one of those people. With Audible time no longer stands in the way between me and knowledge.

Duolingo

Another app that I have is Duolingo. The app helps you learn a foreign language easily with minimum daily effort. Although the best way to learn anything is to immerse yourself, if you don't have the time to learn a new language you need this app. You can start straight away and if you use it daily soon you will notice that your language skills have improved.

HabitBull

HabitBull. it is a tool that gives you the ability to track your habits. You set a number of things that you want to do every so often, for example, every day, every Thursday, every second Wednesday of the month or whatever it might be. In the initial stages of creating a new habit or routine we only need a little distraction not to do something, and the app helps me to stay on track and on top of what I want to do and it helps me to make sure that I invest time every single day in the things that would help me to get to where I want to get to.

fiverr

Another app that you would want to use is fiverr. On fiverr for as little as $5 you can have a task completed.

The return on investment (ROI) from using fiverr can be great. I have used fiverr for various tasks – from flyer design and transcription to research. I use them for tasks that I can't do or tasks that I can, just don't want to. With the transcription example, I could have done that myself. I realised that there are better things I could do with my time; for example, things that will make use of my creativity, or just go for a coffee with a friend. The money is not a lot and it helps you getting used to delegating and valuing your time more.

Buffer

Buffer is a social media scheduling app. It allows you to queue up posts to be automatically shared on your social media profiles. It is useful to help you build a brand across multiple channels when you don't have the time to regularly post. To build social media engagements, you need to post relevant and valuable information to your audience. Your main job afterwards will be to reply to people who have interacted with your posts.

Timetune

Timetune will help you become more aware of where your time goes. You can also plan your ideal week and know what you're aiming for. When I first used it, as mentioned earlier in the book, I was shocked that I didn't know what I was doing with my days. Having that understanding meant that I could take control of my time and reclaim some of it back.

IFTTT

IFTTT (If This Then That) is another automation app that will save you time. IFTTT looks for certain criteria to be met for it to then complete an action. The criteria could be if the weather forecast for tomorrow is rain the app could text you to remind me to get an umbrella. Or if someone sends me a message from one platform that I don't change very often, I could set the system to send me a message on a platform that I do check. or if the official date for the new Star Wars movie is announced message me as I want to find out straight away, but I don't want to constantly have to check for it. This is the power of automating simple tasks and letting a piece of software be on the lookout for things that are relevant to you instead of you searching on a regular basis and not getting any results. You could use this tool as leverage because as already mentioned you don't have to be there in person and do all the heavy lifting, let the robots do that for you. You could link this app to your home assistant and could automate things. This way you could have shopping lists automatically added to your calendar or to your Toodledo or send a text message. The two could keep a record of the songs that have been played via the home assistant.

Eventbrite / Meetup / Facebook

You can use Eventbrite, Meetup.com and Facebook to both, attend and organise events. When you attend an event, the organiser has specified the time, place and price, if any. There are hundreds of events organised across the world, which give you the chance to find an event on a topic you're interested in. There are plenty of free high-value seminars you can attend to get some information. Remove the phrases "I don't know how to do this" or "I don't know anyone who does this" from your vocabulary. With Google, Eventbrite, Meetup.com and Facebook, you can find all the information you need to at least start that new venture. Look for events on the topic and you'll be sure to find at least one that is close to you, and free. Of course, if you can afford to pay, then you can go to even more events. The idea of the events is to get systemised knowledge on a subject. This can save you time on research.

You can also use the platforms as an event organiser. Use it to promote your business, or to organise a local book club.

Quuu Promote

This is a social media promotional tool that you can use to boost the reach of your content. It is a way to promote your content to influencers. There's no longer the excuse that no one knows about you and you can't get the reach you need. Sometimes you need to speculate to accumulate. Use Quuu Promote to kick-start your online visibility and start building up your audience. Get hundreds of shares, mentions and clicks.

#journoreqest

This is a hashtag within Twitter that allows you to get in touch with journalists who are already writing on a particular subject. They look for people to reach out to and discuss the subject. This is great when you are building a business because you have the opportunity to get in touch with journalists and to help them write the article. This will get your name in the article and will help you build a relationship with the journalist which you can use later on. It will allow you to appear in various publications which will build your credibility and portray you as the authority in a certain field.

Conclusion

As you can see, most of those tools and apps are eliminating any excuses you may have. You can no longer say that, and be truthful, "I don't have time to read or to learn a language". Now the only question you should have is what you want, not how to get it. The other reason to use the tools is so you don't have to remember everything, or to spend time doing something. If a robot (any piece of software) can do something for you, let it. Your time can be better spent elsewhere. The key to successful use of technology is to be aware of what your excuses are and preempt them.

EPILOGUE

Congratulations for finishing this book! You are now equipped with the knowledge and tools to boost your productivity, to excel in your career and your life. You now have the understanding of how easy things could be when you put your mind to it. Now you know why marketing matters and how to use it to your advantage!

Printed in Great Britain
by Amazon